YORKSHIRE POST

YORKSHIRE

IN PARTICULAR

AN ALTERNATIVE A–Z

FOREWORD BY GERVASE PHINN

EDITED BY MICHAEL HICKLING

Contributors: Jill Armstrong, Chris Berry, Bill Bridge, Duncan Hamilton, Grace Hammond, Sheena Hastings, John Ledger, Frederick Manby, David Overend, Stephanie Smith, Andrew Vine, Alex Wood.

GREAT NORTHERN

Great Northern Books Limited
PO Box 213, Ilkley, LS29 9WS

www.greatnorthernbooks.co.uk

© Yorkshire Post 2007

ISBN: 978 1 905080 34 2

Layout: David Burrill

Printed in Spain

CIP Data

A catalogue for this book is available from the British Library

Contents

From first to last: the essence of a county and its people

I was surprised and delighted when I was asked by The *Yorkshire Post* to write the foreword to this splendid book, which celebrates in the most informative and entertaining way, the very special character of Yorkshire. Within these pages is a treasure house of fascinating details about the people and places, the industries and activities, the history and customs in a county, which boasts more acres within its borders than words in the King James' Bible.

All my life has been spent in Yorkshire and I could not conceive of living and working anywhere else. My parents were typical of many Yorkshire folk: industrious, good humoured, kindly and plain speaking with strong views and a wry sense of humour. You might expect them to have a wry sense of humour, calling a child born in a small red brick semi in Rotherham, Gervase.

As a child I grew up surrounded by Yorkshire people: generous to a fault, hard working but with a blunt nature and fierce honesty. As a teacher in Sheffield and Doncaster and a schools inspector in North Yorkshire, I encountered many comical, forthright children and shrewd, good-natured and dedicated teachers who possessed in abundance that typical Yorkshire dry humour. You will meet many of these characters in the pages of this A-Z.

I still feel that huge sense of awe for 'God's Own Country.' Yorkshire is a county of infinite variety and, to my mind, the scenery is the most stunning in the British Isles. The county might not embrace within its sprawling borders the vast magnificence of the Scottish Highlands or the towering grandeur of Snowdonia, but there is a particular beauty in each of its diverse landscapes.

The great and vastly underrated Yorkshire writer Laurence Sterne, the author of Tristram Shandy, wrote in his 'Letter to Eliza' of 1767:

Yorkshire … 'O 'tis a delicious retreat both from its beauty and air of Solitude; and so sweetly does every thing about it invite your mind to rest from its Labours and be at peace with itself and the world.'

Yorkshire is indeed 'a delicious retreat' and attracts people from all over the world.

'I think one of the reasons why one loves a

"All my life has been spent in Yorkshire and I could not conceive of living and working anywhere else."

holiday in Yorkshire,' wrote Harold Macmillan in 1966 in a letter to Lady Swinton thanking her for her hospitality, *'is that in a confused and changing world, the picture in one's mind is not spoilt. If you ever go to Venice or Florence or Assisi, you might as well be at Victoria Station – masses of tourists, chiefly Germans in shorts. If you go to Yorkshire, the hills, the keepers, the farmers, the farmers' sons, the drivers are the same; and there is a sense of continuity. There is also the country and neighbourliness that goes with the people who live in this remote and beautiful county.'*

Yorkshire is indeed 'beautiful' but it is the proud, plain speaking people who make the county so very special. I love the warmth of spirit, the kindness, the unflagging hospitality and courage of my fellow Yorkshiremen and women, with their sharp humour and shrewd down to earth insight into human nature. 'Never ask a Yorkshireman if he's from Yorkshire,' goes the traditional saying. 'If he is, he'll tell you anyway. If he's not you'll only embarrass him.'

Gervase Phinn

ABDICATION

In 1936 the King of England was having an affair with a divorced woman who was possibly a German agent and was sleeping with at least one other man, a second-hand car salesman. The British public was shut out of this story until the *Yorkshire Post* opened the door. A gale swept through, and Edward VIII, a reluctant monarch in any event, was blown away. The man who set in motion this extraordinary sequence was the former Wool Textiles correspondent of the *Yorkshire Post*, Harry Franz. Early on the afternoon of December 1, young Harry was sent to walk over to the home of Dr Alfred Blunt, the Bishop of Bradford, to collect some copy. The Bishop had written out the presidential address he was about to give to the Bradford Diocesan Conference, and Harry dutifully carried it back to his newsroom. All routine stuff. But Arthur Mann, the editor of the *Yorkshire Post*, believed he detected, in the Bishop's reference to the forthcoming coronation of Edward VIII, a coded warning to the King about his relationship with Mrs Wallis Simpson – the affair which all Fleet Street knew about but had voluntarily agreed not to publish. The leader article printed in next day's *Yorkshire Post* was picked up by the rest of the press, the story was out, and within days Edward VIII had abdicated. **MH**

AIDENSFIELD

Known to the real people who live there as Goathland, this has been the setting for Heartbeat since its comforting Sunday evening presence first filled our television screens on April 10, 1992. Now big in Iran apparently, where the mullahs endorse its values (makes a change from taking British hostages), there can hardly be any place in the world which does not warm to these tales of a young constable who quits London in the 1960s for a gentler beat on the North York Moors. Peter Walker (Nicholas Rhea), author of the original books, based them on his own experiences and still lives – and writes – nearby at Ampleforth. His ex-colleagues have also shared in the fruits of *Heartbeat's* success, signing up for years of voluntary overtime, policing the film set and its imaginary bobbies. **MH**

AIRE

It is hard to fault a river. It does its job, draining the land into a lake or a sea. The Aire, the longest river in Yorkshire, is by no means the loveliest. It rises in magnificent limestone country at Malham, in the Yorkshire Dales National Park and what better start could any river want? The village gives its name to Malhamdale, robbing the

People stroll through Kirkstall Abbey estate by the River Aire on an autumn afternoon

Aire of its own titular dale until it reaches Skipton and heads towards Keighley and Shipley. By Skipton we have seen the best of the river, which degenerates in beauty as it passes Leeds and Castleford. At historic Snaith, south of Selby, the river is rather unlovely, its waters a muddy blur as it passes baronial Carleton Towers, feeling the effects of the tidal Ouse, which it joins a few miles further on at Airmyn. Here, steel bulwarks prevent it overflowing into the roads on either side.

Yorkshire Water has been praised for cleaning up the Aire, a river once so noxious that just falling in to one of the industrial stretches could result in life-threatening illness. In Malham's headwaters are crayfish and trout. Porpoises have been seen in the tidal mouth, an indication that there are healthy fish stocks.

I have lived on or near the Aire for most of my life and do not expect to move away. I see it every morning, across the road, as it threads through the stepping stones that

Craig Witty, the brewer at Daleside Brewery, Starbeck.

connect the upper village green with its left-bank sibling. It is lovely here, a compensation for the thundering trucks. In spring snowdrops are replaced by hundreds of daffodils. In summer children will arrive full of hope with floppy fishing nets.

It gets better still as we follow it north through harmonious Bell Busk, where oyster catchers shriek and curlews spend their summer. Near curious Eel Ark Hill it is joined by the Pennine Way footpath, which from now on accompanies it through Airton, arguably the nicest stretch, into Malham village. This short nice bit of just six or seven miles is why the Aire does not rank with the Ure and Swale and Wharfe and Ribble, all of which have the indulgence of longer valleys and drops in terrain in which to show off their rapids and falls and umbrous pools. **FM**

ALE

Few things are closer to a Yorkshireman's heart than a pint of golden, hoppy beer. The county boasts more breweries than anywhere else in the country – more than 70 breweries compared to 16 in the early 1970s, when the Campaign for Real Ale was founded. Ale has been served in Yorkshire ever since the locals discovered the miracle of fermenting yeast, hops and water, but the real history of producing it here started in 1758 when the Hartley family founded a brewery at Tadcaster. That brewery was taken over by John Smith in 1852, who was funded by his father, Samuel, a cattle dealer and butcher, from Leeds. After a family rift, a new brewery was established next door. The John Smith and Samuel Smith breweries survive as monuments to the beginnings of brewing. Others have not been so lucky. The Wards and Whitbread breweries in Sheffield have gone, as has Darley's at Thorne. But Tetley, set up in Leeds in 1822, lives on and

prospers, as do such other historic names as Timothy Taylor, at Keighley, and Theakston, in Masham. Such names have been joined by a legion of smaller breweries, often run by people who learned their trade with the big boys, producing wonderful ales, such as Daleside, from Harrogate, named best beer in the *Yorkshire Post Taste Awards*. But is there such a thing as a characteristic Yorkshire ale? Barrie Pepper, former chairman of the British Guild of Beer Writers, and author thinks so. "They have a hoppiness and a lot of mouth feel," he says. "There's a paleness of colour, too. Sam Smith's is a bit darker and bit more malty, but a lot of the others like Taylor's and Old Mill, or some of the smaller ones like Daleside are less than a deep gold – more a pale gold. It is possible to do a hop count of beer, and I would say that it's high in most of the Yorkshire beers." **AV**

APPLES

Ashmead's Kernel, Howgate Wonder, Lord Lambourne, Orleans Reinette, Lanes Prince Albert.... the names are chalked up above the boxes of apples being stored in a barn in the orchard at Ampleforth Abbey. The sweet smell makes you want to help yourself to a lovely, juicy apple and bite into it straight away but we are on rather hallowed ground here and anyway, Father Rainer, the monk in charge, keeps a sharp eye on his precious stock. Apples and the abbey have been a long established partnership. When the monks first arrived in the valley in 1802 they grew apple trees, then Abbot Oswald Smith planted more at the beginning of the 20th century. The present orchard has been expanded and remodelled over the years. It covers over two hectares and there are around 2000 trees with 45 varieties cultivated. Some are real veterans like the Ribston Pippin, originating from a tree

Ampleforth's Father Rainer in the orchard of the school. Jim Moran.

Dave Milnes pictured in the Main Gallery at the Staithes Gallery. Simon Hulme.

grown locally at Ribston Hall in the 17th century. People love to visit the orchard because they can find apples they remember from their childhood. They used to be able to just turn up and leave the money for a bag of apples in an honesty box. The monks are trying to be a bit more businesslike now. They still sell the apples from the orchard and they have also started a useful sideline. The apples that aren't good enough to be sold are made into cider, for which there is a waiting list, and cider brandy, available at upmarket stockists. **JA**

ARCADES

There's nothing new about the lure of shopping therapy, especially when it's cosily undercover. In the 18th century metropolitan toffs were the ones with the serious disposable incomes and they flocked to places like the Burlington Arcade to see and be seen. The idea was copied when the Industrial Revolution put spending money in the pockets of a broader class of people. In Leeds in the 1870s Charles Thornton saw an opportunity in the taste of the newly-wealthy West Riding middle classes for luxury goods. At the junction of the Headrow and Briggate he introduced the idea of an arcade where shoppers could promenade, purchase and go to the theatre as well. Seven others quickly followed, all flamboyant embellishments to the city scene and monuments to the acquisitive instinct. Miraculously, considering what happened elsewhere in Yorkshire, four escaped the wrecking balls of philistine developers in the 1970s. By the 1980s – and with the help of admirers like Alan Bennett – they had come to be recognised for what they are, glorious survivors which deserved to be cherished. Instead of knocking them down, a new breed of developer showed at the Victoria Quarter how the arcades could meet the demands of a well-heeled, brand-consuming, 21st century clientele determined to shop until they drop. **MH**

ARTISTS' COLONY

Recreating realistic water on canvas is notoriously difficult. Many brushes have been thrown aside, and canvasses abandoned by artists defeated by the watery challenge. In the 1870s James Hook, regularly visited Clovelly on the North Devon coast to paint. Others followed, lured by the promise of a healthier lifestyle and the term "art colony" was born. The new national railway network linked these obscure coastal reaches and at Staithes the trains took away the fish and brought back painters. Their occasional visits turned into lengthy stays and the Staithes Group emerged. Husband and wife Harold and Laura Knight spent 10 years here among what Laura called "the freedom, the austerity, the savagery, the wildness". But the regularity of disasters at sea forced her to quit. She wrote in later life, "I could not contemplate more tragedies" among "the wild race of fisher people I loved so well". By the onset of the First World War the group had ceased to exist. Today's artists have a

new shop window. A couple from York, Dave and Alison Milnes, recently opened the excellent Staithes Gallery on High Street, in a fascinating old building which has its own smugglers' tunnel. **MH**

ASHES

Steve Harmison's first ball at Brisbane probably determined the course of the 2006–7 Ashes series Down Under. A Yorkshire bowler made a bigger mark than that. Step forward Edmund "Ted" Peate of Yeadon, a sturdy Victorian who changed the nature of matches between England and Australia, maybe even the relationship between the Mother Country and her former colony. Ted, regarded as one of the best bowlers in the world, whose spin relied on accuracy rather than turn, was in the team for a fateful one-off Test in 1882. England were 75–9 in their second innings and needed ten to win. Peate, the last man who earlier had taken eight Australian wickets, strode out to partner CT Studd, a recognised batsman. Peate just needed to keep his end up until the target was reached. Instead, to the dismay of his teammates, including WG Grace and 20,000 spectators, he went for glory. He scored two then took a swipe at another delivery from Henry Boyle which hit the stumps. The next issue of *The Sporting Times* carried a mock obituary "In affectionate remembrance of English cricket which died at The Oval on 29 August, 1882. Deeply lamented by a large circle of sorrowing friends and acquaintances. RIP ... The body will be cremated and the Ashes taken to Australia". Cricket's greatest Test contest was born. **MH**

B

BEMPTON CLIFFS

There isn't a more dizzying spot on the Yorkshire coast than Bempton Cliffs, and when the country's biggest colony of seabirds takes wing, not a more spectacular one. The mighty chalk cliffs that soar to more than 400ft from the crashing waves below are among Britain's highest, and to stand on one of the viewing platforms high above the North Sea is not for the faint-hearted. But visitors need to look down, however dizzy they become, because nesting on the cliff face are a quarter of a million seabirds.

Gannets, kittiwakes, guillemots and puffins are all here, in one of the best-loved of all RSPB reserves. The charity looks after a three-mile section of the coastline, and the fields that run up to the cliff edge are full of wildlife and a magnet for birdwatchers hoping for a glimpse of rare migrant buntings and warblers from Eastern Europe.

The cliffs were not always such a haven. In the mid-19th century, a fashion arose for shooting kittiwakes on the cliffs for millinery, and for 200 years, the "climmers" of Bempton claimed their own place as one of the most breathtaking sights on the Yorkshire coast, scaling the cliff-face in search of eggs. Some made their way to the shops and restaurants of the West Riding, but most were sold to the crowds which gathered at the top of the cliffs to watch the daredevils below.

Demand for the eggs soared during the Second World War, when hens' eggs were in short supply. In May 1945, the *Yorkshire Post* noted that kittiwake eggs were going at 2s 6d a dozen, and there was a brisk trade in guillemot eggs at 4s a dozen, though they had been as costly as 6d each earlier in the war.

Conventional wisdom had it that guillemot eggs were best eaten soft-boiled with plenty of salt, pepper and vinegar to mask the slightly fishy taste.

There was, though, a terrible environmental price to pay for the climmers' activities. So many eggs were taken from nests – some estimates put it at 130,000 a year – that the guillemot population went into decline. The bell tolled for the climmers in 1954, when the Wild Birds Protection Act came in to force and outlawed the raiding of nests. By then, the shooters in search of kittiwake feathers were gone, too, and the birds could once again nest in peace. **AV**

BENNETT, ALAN

"I note at the age of 10 a fully-developed ability not to quite enjoy myself, a capacity I have retained intact ever since." That line – from *Telling Tales*, his memoir of childhood in Leeds – is the quintessential Alan Bennett: humbly laconic, self-deprecating, and

Bempton Cliffs.

Alan Bennett

saturnine and also concealing behind its dry humour as much as it reveals. Bennett, born in 1934, has an ear for dialogue as good as Mozart's ear for a note of music. It is transparent in a body of work (so consistently fine it almost defies belief) for stage, page and screen that is sensitive and perceptive in revealing the nuances – and often the aching sadnesses – of ordinary life without ever dissolving into sentimentality. Bennett's characters are primarily people who tolerate, often by way of denial, humdrum or plain grey existences, such as those portrayed in the monologues *A Woman of No Importance*, *Intensive Care* and *A Cream Cracker Under the Settee*. His comedy is rooted in close observation of everyday circumstances, the features of which are, like a mirror held to the face, instantly recognisable. No other writer captures as

vividly as Bennett the pitfalls and struggles, and the personal vanities and social pretensions, of the striving for working or middle-class respectability. Although he lives in London – sleeping in the bed in which he was born – Bennett has a home in the Yorkshire Dales, talks with a Yorkshire accent and continues to write about Yorkshire and his family in books, among them *Writing Home* (1994) and *Untold Stories* (2005). Untold Stories includes the tender account of the Alzheimer's disease which affected his mother and the stark essay of his own diagnosis and treatment for cancer. The prose is always so beautiful, and the content so striking, that Bennett emerges as that rare thing – both a literary figure and a popular one in regard to his readership. It is a perfectly safe wager that Bennett will be read and equally admired a century from now.

"I'm not happy but not unhappy about it," says one of Bennett's History Boys in response to a question about how he views his life. You sincerely hope that such a half-lament of a reply isn't autobiographical. Bennett gives so much pleasure to others that he deserves to be supremely happy himself. **DH**

BETJEMAN'S CHURCHES

Just a little shame-facedly, Sir John Betjeman once confessed that he loved some buildings more than he loved people. And often the architecture that most moved him – lyrically as well as spiritually – were churches. "Without a church, " wrote Betjeman "I think a place lacks its heart and identity." He liked the majestic splendour of a spire, hard-edged and sharp against a cobalt sky. He liked, after pushing open the oak door, to inhale the heavy scent of hymn books and wax and dust. He liked the significant, but often unseen, small detail of a church: a carving, a

John Betjeman in Pontefract, 1970.

bell rope, the worn inscription on a gravestone. Wherever he went, Betjeman sought out churches with notebook in hand. As a champion of Victorian architecture, he was particularly drawn, like a filing to a magnet, to St Andrew at Kirby Grindalythe, one of the earliest churches in the Wolds valley (Kirby means "the place of the church"). It is one of 17 rural churches restored with money from Sir Tatton Sykes, the 5th Baronet (1826–1913). Sir Tatton recruited architect G (George) E (Edmund) Street – later to become Professor of Architecture at the Royal Academy – in 1872 to rebuild the Norman chancel, fashion a marble pulpit and add a new nave in the style of the mid-13th century. The work took three years. In 1893, a mosaic decorated the entire internal West wall. When he saw it, Betjeman was mightily impressed. He was so fond of another architect – Temple Moore –

that he immortalised him in verse in *Perp Revival i' the North*:

O, I wads gang tae Harrogate
Tae a kirk by Temple Moore

The poem celebrates two more Yorkshire churches: St Wilfrid's at Harrogate and St Mary Magdalene, tucked into the North Yorkshire Moors – once so remote that clergy in the Victorian era were obliged to travel overnight and sleep in a hammock strung in the south aisle in time for Sunday service. As Betjeman wrote:

It's a far cry frae Harrogate
And mony a heathery mile
Tae a stane kirk wi' a wee spire
And a verra wee south aisle

DH

BOLLYWOOD IN YORKSHIRE

Abhishek Bachchan and Aishwarya Rai – do these names mean anything to you? Maybe not as much as Tom Cruise or Nicole Kidman but 3.2 billion film-goers worldwide can't be wrong. The couple who have just wed in Mumbai are among the brightest stars in the firmament of India's film industry which is now twice the size of Hollywood's. It's a business worth more than a couple of billion American dollars and turns out over 1,000 pictures a year with budgets up to $20m each.

Understandably, the Indians did not wish to be eclipsed by American glitz and glamour and at the turn of the Millennium introduced their own annual version of the Oscars. The International Indian Film Academy (IIFA) Weekend and the Idea IIFA Awards are now the showcase and shop window for the industry and the opportunity to host them creates something of an international stampede.

After the likes of Johannesburg and Singapore. it was Bradford's turn. The city has capitalised on that huge post-war movement of people from the sub-continent which so changed its culture and complexion. The one-time worsted capital of the world was now the obvious choice to be the temporary capital of the Hindi film industry for four days at the beginning of June 2007. Bradfordians experienced a similar windfall to the one the Dutch enjoyed in 2006 when the Bollywood extravaganza in Amsterdam saw 15,000 visitors book into 12,000 hotel rooms before going out on the town and spending 18.64m euros.

In the longer term, the impact of the event's coverage on 315 million television viewers around the world did no harm to Yorkshire's tourism, or the prospects for doing business with one of the fastest growing economies in the world. **MH**

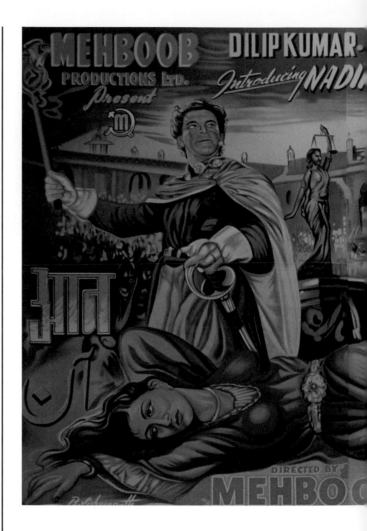

BRIGHT, TIMOTHY

Timothy Bright was a Sheffield man born about 1551 with a fertile mind. Two of the main things that occupied it sit oddly together – medicine and shorthand. For the latter, he wrote a guide which he presented to Queen Elizabeth, who in turn gave him the rich West Yorkshire living of Methley and then Barwick-in-Elmet, where the parishioners didn't like him very much.

Bright heard about William Slingsby

India's film industry is the world's biggest.

who had drunk from a moorland spring near Harrogate and noticed it tasted like the water in Spa(w) in the Ardennes which he had visited. Slingsby had developed the Yorkshire well so the waters could be drunk conveniently for medicinal reasons – possibly a first in England. Timothy Bright endorsed the view that this spring had healing properties and named Harrogate as the "The English Spaw". He was a man whose views carried weight, since he had also been Elizabeth I's physician.

Bright was by no means the first to promote the notion of beneficial water therapies in England. The Romans had been keen too. Nero used "spa" when referring to the Baths of ancient Rome, a term possibly drawn from the Latin acronym for sanitas per aquas (health through water). More springs were discovered and elegant Georgian Harrogate flourished as visitors flooded in prepared to spend money like water. Victorian doctors urged their wealthy patients to come here and they booked into

Brimham Rocks

the new luxury hotels in numbers. The opening on July 23, 1897, by the Duke of Cambridge, of the Royal Baths Assembly Rooms was Harrogate's crowning glory – offering mud baths, steam rooms, hydrotherapy departments, a medicinal waters dispensary and consulting doctors on tap. Its opulent Turkish Baths displayed Islamic-inspired designs that featured sweeping Moorish arches with painted, vaulted ceilings. The terrazzo floors were laid by craftsmen brought over from Italy. It was said that on any morning during the spa season, it was possible to hold a Cabinet meeting at the Pump Room, so many ministers were to be found there. By the early 20th century Harrogate was the UK's leading bottler and exporter of table water.

The revenue streams dried up after the Second World War. The new National Health Service did not send patients for water treatments. A crisis of self-belief climaxed with the Royal Baths Assembly Rooms (although not the Turkish Baths) closing in 1969. Shortly after, water bottling came to an end. Harrogate was quite unprepared for the Evian phenomenon – when it suddenly became the fashion for normally sensible people to pay inordinate sums of money for a small plastic bottle of branded water that had been trucked halfway across Europe. The Continent had kept faith with the feelgood factor of water and its therapies, even if the scientific basis for it health-giving properties was unproven. The Germans in particular adored their 300-odd spas.

Harrogate eventually woke up to the fact that there was money in water once more. A new bottled water operation started competing with Evian and the rest on supermarket shelves and nowhere was the turn-around more complete than at the Turkish Baths. A sad decline was arrested and £1m was spent on restoring the baths' Edwardian glory. It all fits in nicely with today's thirst for keeping in shape. The growth in luxury hotel spas and spa resorts worldwide in the last 10 years has been dizzying and the profits are the handsomest in the hospitality business. Harrogate ought to be sitting pretty as people get more determined to keep up personal appearances and happily part with wads of cash in the attractive, but doomed, quest for the suppleness and lustre of youth. **MH**

BRIMHAM ROCKS

Moulded plastic at playgroup or tubular steel in the back garden are all very well as substitutes go, but if you want to introduce children to the daddy and mummy of all adventures, then squaring up to the might of Brimham Rocks is the most unforgettable experience a youngster can have. Including everything Disney has in the also-rans. Four miles east of Pateley Bridge in North Yorkshire, 10 miles north-west of Harrogate, and 10 miles south-east of Ripon are your pointers. Off the B6165, park in the National Trust car park – cleverly situated so that you don't see the drama and extent of the Rocks from there – and meander up the ferny path with your picnic and pack of children in tow. Children, in-house or borrowed, are a must. Reaching the top, a landscape opens up before you that has been developing into a rocky forest for 320 million years, ever since a huge river washed down grit and sand from granite mountains in northern Scotland and Norway. A delta formed, covering half of Yorkshire. Increasing layers of grit and sand, along with rock crystals of felsdspar and quartz, built up to form the tough sandstone known as Millstone Grit. The exposed sections are seen today as Brimham Rocks.

Beyond monstrous rocks fashioned by the elements into shapes like a dancing bear, a toadstool, a totem pole, kissing birds, and hundreds of others, there is a view to behold towards Summerbridge and Lower Nidderdale. Savour it from the highest flat rock, as the sarnies and crisps are passed around.

Because these outcrops cover about 50 acres, the site never feels crowded, even on the hottest summer day. Let loose at Brimham, city kids instantly discovered their inner Mowgli, clambering (at first falteringly) onto the nearest ledge, and shouting "I'm the king of the castle!" Suddenly they will be Swallows or Amazons and having awfully big adventures. Anything could happen. Someone might get stuck somewhere, as confidence swells. Sometimes a dare is involved. All the parent can do is hope to keep up with them, as they wriggle through gaps where no hips should fit (you have to find a different way round), and try not to be a wimp as they leap from rock to rock like goats. In all our years of visiting, there have been no serious falls or broken limbs. Maybe we've been lucky – but I would never go on a wettish day. **SH**

The enduring appeal of buckets and spades

BUCKET AND SPADE

It's a great pity that Albert Einstein – so far as is known – never visited Filey on a sunny bank holiday for a spot of contemplating, for had he done so the great thinker would surely have formulated another immutable law. Einstein's Theory of the Seaside would have gone something like this: $B + S = D2$, where B is a bucket, S is a spade and D is delight for children, which is multiplied when there's more than one bucket to hand, one for the sand and one for the seawater.

The science of the bucket and spade is complex. Generations of children have grappled with it, and still do. What's the best sand-to-water ratio for sand pies? Can a moat round a castle be connected to the sea? Is using a bucket shaped like a miniature castle cheating? Can dad be buried up to his neck with the spade? How annoyed will dad be if the back of his deckchair is dug around until it collapses?

Whatever the shape, a bucket and spade is as much a part of the seaside as the beach and the sea. They were first sold on the east coast some time in the 1870s, when enterprising manufacturers realised that there was a ready market among the crowds flocking there on the newly-built railways. The rest is history. Countless thousands are still sold at the seaside, and the thrill of mixing sand and seawater, or just digging holes, is as potent for children today as it was 130 years ago. **AV**

CANALS

West Yorkshire textile makers knew there was a big world out there. But they were stuck in the middle of the country. So they pushed a novel idea – shift the goods on water and forget the tracks and wretched roads. Nothing so ambitious had been floated before and an Act of Parliament in 1699 cleared the way. Making the Aire and Calder navigable to link with the Ouse opened up the port of Hull. Textiles started flowing out in 1704 and raw materials from distant parts came back up stream. The waterway ensured the prosperity of Leeds, Wakefield, Castleford, Knottingley and Goole and it formed the eastern side of a through-route between the North Sea and Irish Sea with the Leeds-Liverpool canal. There was a fallout over the route – Liverpudlian merchants wanted the canal to come via Wigan so they could get at the coal. West Yorkshire priorities were the limestone supplies from quarries around Skipton and the shortest route to the Mersey. At 127 miles, it became England's longest single canal although, technically, it was never completed (a section of the Lancaster Canal was used to join it up in 1816). At Bingley, they built Five Rise Locks – the steepest and widest staircase of locks in Britain, where barges came to be raised by 60ft in 100 meters as they bore millions of tons of textiles at a stately pace

out of the West Riding towards the coast and ships waiting to sail west across the world and to Africa.

The trickiest challenge was presented to the canal-building navvies by a company formed in 1793. The line of their route across the Pennine required the carving of a way through solid rock. The Standedge Tunnel, at just over 5,000 metres, would be the longest and highest in the country. But the engineering soon went awry and Thomas Telford was eventually brought in to sort it out. The tunnel cost more than twice the original estimate and took so long that by the time it was complete, other canals were already opened and had pinched its trade. Customers could not expect express delivery. Manpower was the only option. The boats had to be uncoupled from their towing horse prior to the arduous four-hour process of "legging". Mighty thighs were required of the man who had to lie on his back on the boat roof and push against the rock above to get momentum. It took four hours before there was light at the end of the tunnel.

The secret of the canals' success was moving stuff cheaply in bulk – more than a thousand boats worked on the Leeds-Liverpool. But then the railways did it better and lorries finally consigned canals to history and disuse. Local enthusiasts slaved in their spare time to to stave off decay and closure until the tide finally turned in the late 1960s.

The Bingley Five Rise locks on the Leeds-Liverpool Canal

The British rediscovered their canals – this time as places of delight for anglers and for boaters, among them Harrison Ford and Calista Flockhart, who found a top speed of four miles per hour an antidote to rush-hour in Hollywood. Walkers and cyclists venturing on to canal towpaths discovered they were bowling along unique, long distance wildlife corridors. **MH**

CLOGS

I grew up in the 1950s in a village where young lads wore clogs. Mine were made by Meakins of Skipton and I can still remember, 50 years later, the utility of these toughest of shoes. In winter, they were invaluable for breaking the ice on the stream and the snow would pack up inside the clog iron that rimmed the beechwood sole like a horseshoe.

Denis Nelson from Nelson Footwear in Settle demonstrates clog making. Emma Nichols

One tottered along on this icy platform sole until it could be removed – best by kicking a solid object like a stone or tree root.

The leather uppers were hard enough to repel serious damage from a hoof, dropped stone or a pitchfork prong. The boot sides guarded the shin and ankle. You could say they were as tough as old boots. I shall not pretend I wore them all the time but they are the only footwear I remember from that time, other than little boy's sandals. Peter Johnston (forgive me if the surname is inaccurate) wore them all the time. He was as short as me but stocky and the fastest runner among the handful of us, in what was then the farm-based, small community of Draughton. I always reckoned the clogs gave Peter extra pace but I couldn't run quickly in mine. His feet would clatter down the road, on legs like pistons.

Grown up and having left clogs and the village in my memory, I bought my second pair from a clogmaker in Carleton, about whom I was writing an article. It was an impulse purchase in the early 1970s and I used them in the kitchen garden and for odd jaunts into the ghyll above our old farm. There was a shake (crack) in one of the soles, which let in water. Around the same time, I bought a pair of dressy clogs from a maker in Clitheroe. These were green chrome leather with a pattern cut in. The wooden soles were rimmed by rubber. They were low, really a shoe with a wooden sole. Green? Search me.Agood idea at the time, maybe. These decorative, poncy clogs are the type you'll see at the dozens of clog festivals that take place around the country.

There is an annual Clayfest in Skipton, where the attractions in 2007 included

Yorkshire Flatfooting by the dancers known as Sex on Tap. The organisers say that clog dancing probably started in the mills, when workers wearing clogs would tap their feet to the rhythm of the machines. "It's a very precise form of dance, with intricate foot movements tapping out rhythms with heel and toe. The Lancashire style uses mainly toe movements, while the Durham style makes more use of heels". Well, us Draughton lads used heel, toe, anything that could crack, splinter or rent the object being kicked. If I wanted another pair of real clogs, I would go to our last clog factory, which is Walkley Clogs, in Mytholmroyd, West Yorkshire. Its clogs are widely exported and the specific safety clog meets EU standards – which is why the typical Dutch worker may be walking in Walkleys. **FM**

COBLES

They are as much a part of the Yorkshire coast as the wind and the waves, and they have brought fishermen home safe since the time of the Vikings. These are cobles, the sturdy little vessels which have plied the seas off Bridlington, Scarborough, Filey and Whitby for centuries, and still retain the unshakcable trust and affection of all those who sail in them, whether they be professional fishermen or anglers in search of a day's sea-fishing. It's doubtful if many of the hundreds of thousands of visitors who stroll around the harbours at Bridlington and Scarborough, or pass the Coble Landing at Filey on their way to the Brigg realise that the brightly-painted boats embody the very spirit of these coastal communities, and the formidable challenges of coping with the unpredictability of the North Sea. For the roots of the traditional Yorkshire coble go back a very long way. The origins of the design lie in the longboats of the Vikings, and there are references to them in documents about the east coast dating back to at least the 1400s.

These days, the coble would be termed a "design classic", and so it truly is. Although the design historically varies from port to port and builder to builder, the classic coble has a distinctive, deep prow which allows it to be launched from the sands into powerful head seas, sweeping back to a transom stern equipped with a deep, slim rudder that helps hold the boat to the sea. They are clinker built, using overlaid planks for both strength and watertightness. They are not the most elegant of boats, but they are among the toughest. There were once hundreds of cobles under sail or power on the east coast. Now, they are numbered only in their dozens as the travails of the fishing industry have progressively reduced their number. And yet they survive, because as long as people put to sea from often stormy beaches and harbours, the rugged little coble is the best friend they could have. **AV**

COD

Trawlermen gave their lives for it, the poor gave their pennies for it, and Hull thanked God for it. Cod brought wealth, sustenance and sometimes heartache to Yorkshire's greatest port, as the mighty fleet that once headed out to sea from the Humber brought back boatloads of the fish that for so long helped to feed Britain. Athird of all the fish eaten in Britain used to come via Hull, and cod was king. It was cheaper than haddock and a staple of poorer families' diets. There was so much of it in the seas off the east coast in the 18th century that fishermen from all over Britain headed there, and it became such a favourite part of the nation's diet that William Pitt the Elder referred to it as "British gold".

But Britain could eat far more cod than the North Sea could produce, and as stocks dwindled, the trawlers of Hull had to head farther afield, notably to Iceland. At its peak, Hull had the largest distant-water fleet in the world, with more than 150 vessels fishing for cod, often in appalling conditions that cost lives. Back in port, more than 50,000 jobs depended on the cod the boats brought home.

The Cod Wars were to end all that. Ugly skirmishes between Britain and Iceland were resolved by an uneasy peace deal in 1976, and it was to mark the beginning of the end for the great Hull fleet. These past 30 years haven't been easy for the fishing community, or for cod. The number of trawlers has dwindled to just a few, and the North Sea's cod stocks have become so depleted that the remaining fishermen face crippling restrictions on how much they catch.

Yet the nation's love affair with this ugly fish continues, and its scarcity has seen its price soar. But for all that, cod doesn't put much food on the tables of Hull any more. **AV**

CO-OP

Just as those who served in the Armed Forces never forgot their serial number, those of us brought up with a Co-op at the bottom of the street never let slip their "divvy" digits: the payment of the dividend was always a welcome addition to the family funds. Our Co-op was a lifeline in the days when supermarkets were in the future and your average grocer and baker charged top prices. It was a convenience store before the phrase had been invented. The roots lie in the early days of the 19th century.

The first co-operation in Huddersfield – the Co-operative Trading Association – came together in 1829. It limited itself to a

maximum of 250 members and worked to a motto taken from the book of Isaiah: "They helped everyone his neighbour and everyone said to his brother, be of good courage." They dealt mainly in furnishings, clothing, wool and fancy goods, trading their products for those from other societies, and in 1830 employed their first salesman who was paid 20 shillings (£1) a week.

Huddersfield became the fulcrum of co-operation and it was here that likeminded members of a society which had been established in Rochdale came for advice. Rochdale's final dividend was to become the present home of United Co-operatives, the largest regional society in the country with a turnover of £2.6bn and 18,000 employees. The main businesses of the society are food (biggest operator of convenience stores in the North), travel, motors, health care and funeral services. They are talking about joining the Manchester-based Co-operative Group to create the largest consumer co-operative society in the world. As always, the members will decide. **BB**

COUNTRY SHOWS

Being the biggest British county, Yorkshire naturally has more country shows. Traditionally, the major agricultural gatherings start at Otley in May and finish at Pateley Bridge in September. In July, the centrepiece is at Harrogate for the Great Yorkshire Show. It has yet to add the word Royal to its title but it is an event as fit for kings and queens as it is for commoners, aristocrats, gentry, the merely filthy rich, the farmhand, moorkeeper. Dog handlers and cake makers mingle with show jumpers and bee keepers. There's much mingling on the showfield, too. Once, these shows would offer a rare, perhaps only annual, opportunity to say hello to someone. Mobile

Observers and a competitor at Kilnsey Show

phones and the internet have shrunk the planet but they are nothing like the real thing, face-to-face contact. Malham and Kilnsey vie for the best setting. Malham has the distant backcloth of the renowned Cove, Kilnsey is almost under the shadow of the beaky Crag. Gargrave, however, is in a gentleman's park, and if the rain spares us, it can look very good. As a visitor, you can check the achievements of cake makers and bean growers. You can enter races which take

you up and down the fells. You can watch cricket at Pateley Show, or you may enter your dog or yourself in some competition.

The only thing I ever won was seven shillings and sixpence and a drink after beating a Malhamdale farmer's stockman up and down the pole in a show tent (two poles, I was in my prime, and the judgment of farmer and hired hand may have been clouded by gin and Theakston's respectively). The main thing is that you don't need to behave badly to enjoy any of these shows. In fact, I'd advise against it. Getting to just one will give the stranger an insight into the rural community, how it works and who works there. **FM**

CRICKET AT SCARBOROUGH

...in Festival week

Is there a more beautiful phrase in the English language than: "Cricket at Scarborough"? Not for a Yorkshireman who loves cricket and Scarborough. Those three words are sufficient to create an image so vivid and perfect that it could be framed and hung like a painting: the swell of foam from North Sea summer waves, the squawk of gulls in swooping mid-flight, the North Marine Road Ground sealed in baking heat; white and sea-green striped tents, deckchairs in primary colours; sun-burnt faces; a flag coiled around the flagpole on a breathless morning.

Ritual attaches itself easily to watching cricket at Scarborough, and a sense of ceremony accompanies it, too: the slow walk to the match – preferably taking in a sea view; the lumpen bag choked with food and drink and all the accoutrements necessary for a day's cricket – books and newspapers and pens and a portable radio. The first drink of the day is taken just as the clock nudges past noon. At lunch, the bag is unpacked and a solemn inspection of the pitch – swept, rolled and re-marked – takes place. Across the outfield, a hundred games are being played with seaside bats and balls. And late in the afternoon, there's a final effort to finish the *Yorkshire Post* crossword.

Repetition never dulls this familiar routine. "Whenever a pilgrimage through the cricketer's England may begin it must surely end, if the traveller have any sense of the appropriate, at Scarborough in Festival time," wrote JM Kilburn. Cricket correspondent of the *Yorkshire Post* for 40 years, Kilburn captured the essence of the week more exquisitely than anyone before or since.

"Cricket on holiday," was his description of it. "Scarborough is always new yet never changes," he added, surveying the cliff separating the bays, the Norman Castle, the hotels and boarding houses, the spread of sand, the Spa and the harbour. Interrupted only by the war years, the Scarborough festival has run since 1876 and its history is intertwined with cricket's golden names: Grace and Bradman, Boycott and Hutton.

But the matches – whether run feasts or wicket laden – are somehow secondary to the experience of merely being there. Kilburn – who else? – explained it without flaw: "Once visited, Scarborough takes hold of you inexorably... the spell is laid never to be broken." **DH**

CUTTING EDGE

Sheffield's coat of arms, granted in 1843, features Thor and Woden, each with an arm resting on a shield. The mythical gods smiled on an area blessed with coal, ironstone and rivers to drive the waterwheels. Spanish iron, for a sharp edge, was unloaded at Bawtry and the tool and cutlery makers could absorb the cost because they had skilled workers and high quality grindstones driven by the fast-flowing rivers. By the mid-18th century, the Sheaf, Don, Rivelin, Porter and Loxley averaged between three and six waterpowered wheels per mile. Around 1740, Benjamin Huntsman, a clockmaker in Doncaster, invented cast steel – the most important discovery ever made in Sheffield.

At the same time, cutler Thomas Boulsover invented the process of plating copper with a thin layer of silver known as

Metal grinding in Sheffield. Chris Lawton

Sheffield plate. By 1850, the city was making 90 per cent of Britain's steel and Joseph Rodgers became the world's largest cutlery company keeping the "little mesters" going at his or her special skill, whether grinding a blade, polishing it, applying a handle. The inscription "Made in Sheffield" was an even bigger winner when local metallurgist Harry Brearley invented stainless steel.

The city's edge was later dulled by ferocious competition from Far East cutlery makers and for a time it seemed that Thor and Woden might be better depicted pushing a shopping trolley at Meadowhall. But the core industry, even after savage cut-backs, has since risen again to become a world player in specialist steels. **FM**

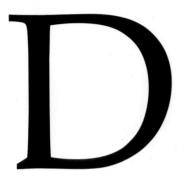

DALES

The Dales of Yorkshire are some of Britain's finest landscape. In the bottom of each valley there is a river, often giving its name to the dale: Airedale, Ribblesdale, Swaledale. There are many exceptions. Wensleydale takes its name from the once important village of Wensley, and its river is the Ure. Littondale is also named after a village, and its river is the Skirfare. Dentdale has a similar naming structure. Langstrothdale, through which the young Wharfe splashes to enter its namesake dale, gets its name from the Vikings, as does Kingsdale, near Ingleton. The majestic dales, unsullied by major towns for most of their length, are Swaledale and Wensleydale, which run west to east across North Yorkshire. Wharfedale, which runs southerly, runs out of dales landscape by Ilkley. The Nidd should be mentioned, too, but the thing is: which is Yorkshire's finest dale? How can we judge? Of the "big" Dales I am leaning more and more towards Wensleydale, but why I can't quite say. Of the boutique dales I have always had a soft spot for Deepdale, which feeds into Dentdale. In summer it is lush and exciting as views open up round each corner. A grandmother was a Fothergill, from this area. She used to roll hardboiled eggs down the hillside with us. A brother's house (there were 13 children) had a porch bristling with walking sticks made from hedgerow hazel. The Dee runs over flat bedrock. Sandpipers skip briskly through the shadows. My father and his friend Walter would come back from a night in Dentdale with a salmon or two. As dales go, it has all I need: beauty, memories, magic. **FM**

DARLEY ARABIAN

Arab influence in the racing business today is largely centred on the enormously rich families who own top-class horses and the Dubai racecourse which stages some of the sport's most lucrative races. At the beginning, three Arabs played pivotal roles in the breeding of thoroughbred racehorses for over 300 years.

The Byerley Turk, the Godolphin Arabian and the Darley Arabian were all stallions imported into England from the Middle East. These were the fathers of racing. All thoroughbreds – and over 110,000 of them born every year worldwide – are descended from one of these three and the greatest of them was the Darley Arabian. Probably foaled about 1700, the horse was purchased by Thomas Darley in Aleppo, Syria, and brought home to Aldby Park, Buttercrambe, North Yorkshire, the Darley Arabian's bloodline is the most popular among stallions, largely through a horse called Bartlett's Childers, who was sired by the Darley Arabian and whose great-grandson was Eclipse, winner of 18 races and sire of three Derby winners. It is estimated that over 80 per cent of thoroughbreds can trace their descent to Eclipse, including Northern Dancer. Eclipse's descendants beat off fierce competition from those of the Byerley Turk to become established as the line of choice for breeders and as the fashion in racing changed from matches over distances up to four miles to much shorter races, including the St Leger, the Derby and the Oaks, and the demand rose for larger, faster, quicker-maturing offspring the Darley Arabian established its supremacy. Records of the breeding of every thoroughbred are meticulously kept with the General Stud Book, first published by Weatherby's in 1791, setting a pattern which is followed all over the world. Any horse whose family lines cannot be traced in the stud books cannot be deemed a thoroughbred. Only those with bloodlines going back to the three original stallions can run in the great races – the Classics – and Yorkshire has the oldest of them all, the St Leger. First run at over two miles at Cantley Common in 1776 – five years after Eclipse retired to stud – the St Leger was the idea of Anthony St Leger and was organised by the second Marquess of Rockingham whose Allabucalia won the inaugural race. The St Leger moved to Town Moor in 1779 and returned to its traditional home in 2007 after being run at York the previous year while redevelopment work was in progress on Town Moor. York is another major centre of racing in Yorkshire – staging important races including the Juddmonte International, the Yorkshire Cup, the Yorkshire Oaks, the Dante Stakes, a major trial for the Derby itself, and the Gimcrack Stakes – and made a major impact when successfully hosting the Royal Ascot meeting of 2005 while the Berkshire course was undergoing major building work.

But racing in Yorkshire is not confined to the grandeur of Doncaster and York. With seven other racecourses in the region, Yorkshire race-goers are almost spoilt for choice, Beverley, Ripon, Thirsk, Pontefract, Redcar, Catterick and Wetherby all offering excellent facilities, thrilling races and great days and evenings out. And in every race, whatever the distance or discipline, there will be horses whose family will be traceable to one of the three great Arabs. **BB**

DAWSON, GREGORY

aka JB Priestley

A note to the reader in JB Priestley's 1946 novel *Bright Day* states emphatically: "This work is pure fiction, containing no autobiographical material ... I beg the reader to accept this not as a mere formality but as a solemn assurance." The obvious conclusion, nonetheless, is that JBP protested too much. The central character in *Bright Day* is Gregory Dawson. He once worked in a wool office (as Priestley did). He became a writer (as Priestley did). He lives in Bruddersford (loosely disguised as the smoky landscape of Priestley's Bradford). Even Dawson's bookish bedroom in Brigg Terrace is drawn from the one Priestley describes as his own in Margin Released. Priestley regarded *Bright Day* as his favourite and most technically successful novel. His fellow Bradfordian writer – and biographer – John Braine thought it "roughly comparable" to David Copperfield. Dawson takes refuge in a Cornish hotel to finish a screenplay. He meets Malcolm and Eleanor Nixey, a couple who slipped out of his life more than three decades previously. This fierce bite of memory carries Dawson/Priestley back "home" – to Bruddersford and to his younger self in an idyllic period before the slaughter of the First

Wensleydale, one of the major dales of Yorkshire that does not take its name from a river.

It is the River Ure that can be seen at the bottom right of this picture.

World War. "There is magic in the countryside, magic in the city; and, over and above it all, magic in people, " he says of Bruddersford. It is impossible to read the book without thinking of Ian Judd's bronze statue. Priestley inspects Bradford from a granite plinth, his long coat caught in the wind, a studious but benevolent expression across his face.

He was a literary perpetual motion machine, the author of fiction, plays, essays, radio broadcasts and polemics. But from his millions of words, the quotation chiselled on to his statue comes from *Bright Day* and begins: "Lost in the smoky valleys . . ." In truth, Priestley never really left them. **DH**

DIVING

The sea may possibly be clear, more often it is murky. There may be no current at all, or it may be running like a train. Above all, you never know what you may find. Most people assume it is too dark, too dirty and too downright dangerous diving off the East Coast. In fact, it offers some of the best diving in the country – even if sometimes you don't know you're on the wreck, until you've actually banged into it. There are thousands of shipwrecks. Many overwhelmed by long-forgotten storms are still unknown, lying buried under the silt. Those visited by recreational divers are mostly victims of enemy action and accident in the two World Wars. People think of submarine warfare as something that happened out in the Atlantic, but it was actually pioneered in the shallow waters off our coast. These wartime wrecks have been reduced to their keels by salvage work, or blown up where they have represented a danger to shipping. Beam trawlers and the forces of Nature have done the rest. Sites range from the largest wreck, the

JB Priestley

Former world champion Dock Pudding maker, Owen Coalville.

14,294–tonne *Pilsudski* which struck a mine off Withernsea en route to Australia in November 1939, to the steamer *Cadmus*, torpedoed by a German submarine, in October 1917. Eighteen-pounder shell cases from the Western Front made up most of the cargo and there are still hundreds scattered about, a poignant reminder of the scale of slaughter. One of the most beautiful and surprising wrecks is the *Lightship* – adorned from bow to stern with marvellous white, orange and pink soft corals. Although she's been submerged some six decades, her tower still stands proud, although the glass is long gone. Further north, somewhere off Flamborough Head, lies the *Bonhomme Richard*. In the evening of September 23, 1779, during the Revolutionary Wars, *HMS Serapis* took on the frigate *Bonhomme Richard* captained by John Paul Jones, father of the United States Navy who had come raiding for merchant ships up the East Coast. They fought at point-blank range for almost four hours. Half the crews on both sides died. *Serapis* was captured but had damaged *Bonhomme Richard* so severely she sank in 180 feet of water. Whoever finds the spot will have found gold. **AW**

DOCK PUDDING

Polygonum bistorta is a spinach-like leaf also known as snakeweed, patience dock and sweet dock, which is recommended for diarrhoea in children because its soothes the digestive tract. It is also good for haemorrhoids and as the main ingredient in dock pudding. When it was plentiful, it used to appear in Calderdale breakfasts and the annual World Dock Pudding Championship is still hosted in April at Mytholmroyd Community and Leisure Centre. In 2007 Robbie Coltrane, of *Cracker* and *Harry Potter* fame, tried his hand. He beat four world champions, but had to concede the pudding crown to another first-time entrant, Darren Kaye. Darren planned to defend his title in April 2008, and to challenge him you will require oatmeal, young nettle tops, a small knob of butter, spring onions and bacon fat. Boil with the onions in a little water until tender, add seasoning and sprinkle in the oatmeal. Boil again for 10 minutes, stirring all the time. Add the butter. Leave overnight. Next morning fry large spoonfuls of the mixture in hot bacon fat and serve with bacon. **MH**

DRESSES OF

Charlotte Brontë

The chief quibble among contemporary authors (well, apart from money, agents and publishers) is that critics focus too much on the writer and not sufficiently on the work. But this isn't a modern day pre-occupation at all. The hard sell on writers' lives properly began or, at least, gathered pace as soon as Elizabeth Gaskell's *The Life of Charlotte Brontë* arrived on shelves in 1857. Whatever the flaws and prejudices of the book – such as its damningly mean portrait of father Patrick –

Charlotte Brontë

The Brontë Parsonage Museum in Haworth.

Mrs Gaskell profitably yoked the hard geographical fact of physical landscape to fictional characters. The Brontë family were characters in a plot that contained almost everything: hardship, loneliness, sacrifice, beauty, love, premature death and mystery – and all of it wrapped in an intriguing Gothic-style setting. Gaskell's book persuaded readers that an uncomfortably rickety journey to Haworth would add to the appeal of what Brontë wrote and provide an insight – or at least throw out some clues – about how and why her books were written. Muddy feet soon beat paths across Ponden Kirk and Top Withens, drinkers ordered pots of ale in the Black Bull and the church pews became worn smooth by the backsides of eager day-trippers. A tourist industry took strong root. Today's literary pilgrim still finds the look and feel of the Parsonage fascinatingly authentic; as though the family have just slipped out for a few hours. Whether it is furniture or jewellery, letters or manuscripts, the collection of personal possessions brings the 19th century alive. But the most unforgettable exhibit brings Charlotte specifically into focus. It is her dresses. The museum owns four of them and alternates its display.

Whichever one the visitor sees – the summer dresses (one with tiny flower prints, the other with a paisley print), the plain dull brown (probably originally purple) or the "going away dress" (worn on honeymoon after her marriage to Arthur Bell Nicholas) the impact is always the same: how startlingly tiny and frail and child-like Charlotte must have been. The waist is tiny, like a doll's, and the arms are pencil thin. You think a strong wind might snap her in two. The measurements of the dresses make the great novelist 4ft 9 or 4ft 10 tall. Add flesh to the slight figure, with the description offered by her publisher George Smith – "She was very small and had a quaint old-fashioned look. Her head seemed too large for her body. She had fine eyes, but her face was marred by the shape of the mouth and by the complexion" – and it's possible to see Charlotte industrious at her writing desk or walking with baby steps around the cobbled village. After her death in 1855, the Brontës' servant, Martha Brown, was gifted the dresses. The first tourists glimpsed them as soon as the The Brontë Society's first museum opened above the Yorkshire Penny Bank at the top of Main Street in 1895. **DH**

DYSON'S CLOCK

If you were "courting" in Leeds, especially pre and immediately post-war, there was an incentive to be on time for your date. For the object of your besotted affection would invariably be waiting beneath Dyson's ornately-decorated clock on Lower Briggate, and every movement of its thick hands on a Roman numeral face was eagerly, and sometimes nervously, monitored. Woe betide, anyone who kept slovenly time in pursuit of love.

The first, cast-iron clock was installed in 1865 when Victorian jeweller John Dyson bought two cottages.

The second beside it – smaller and double-faced – commemorates the birthday of Dyson's wife. It is crowned by Father Time with his scythe, hourglass and wings and was – and remains – a dating landmark in the city. The gilt was added in perfect verse.

Poet Tony Harrison's evocative *Under the Clock* celebrates his mum and dad's early spooning, and the way in which the routine of meeting there as incipient romance and hand-holding led to love and a lifetime of devotion.

*Under Dyson's clock in Lower Briggate
was where my courting parents used to meet
It had a Father Time and Tempus Fugit
sticking out sideways into the street*

Written after his parents' death,
Harrison's poem goes on, sadly: "those
lovers won't meet under it any more".

The poem ends as he contemplates the
"padded boxes" containing his parents'
wedding rings.

It is one of a body of impressive
autobiographical poems about his working
class upbringing. Born in Leeds in 1937,
Harrison won a scholarship to Leeds
Grammar and read classics at Leeds
University.

His parents could scarcely believe that,
from an inarticulate family, he emerged as a
poet. Their bewilderment, like so much else,
was turned into another poem.

*How you became a poet's a mystery!
Wherever did you get your talent from?
I say: I had two uncles, Joe and Harry –
one was a stammerer, the other dumb.*

The story is true. For what fuelled
Harrison was his craving for eloquence and
articulacy – a gift, he says, that he wanted
"more than any other". Without Dyson's
clock, we would not have been able to enjoy
it. **DH**

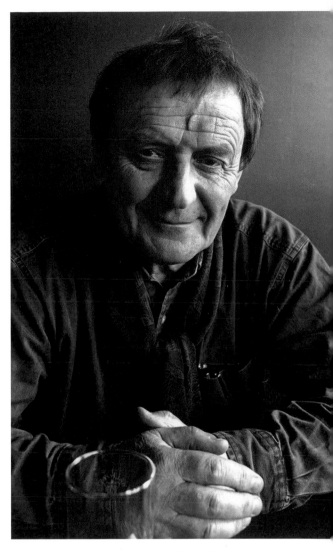

Poet-writer Tony Harrison.

EMLEY MOOR

You can see it from the M1 shortly after passing Barnsley heading north and you know you are nearly home. You can see it from Dick Hudson's public house on the edge of Ilkley Moor and you know we are in for a fine day. And you can see its works any time you turn on the television. The transmission mast at Emley Moor between Huddersfield and Wakefield is more than just a landmark and a brilliant example of late 20th century building technique, it is a part of the fabric of Yorkshire. The tip of the mast is almost 2,000ft above sea level and it is the tallest free-standing structure in the British Isles at a height of 1,084ft (330.4m), but it is its history which helped propel Emley Moor into folklore, more precisely the evening of March 19, 1969. The first mast on Emley Moor stood only 445ft (135m) and was erected to provide pictures from the infant ITV to the Yorkshire region. That structure was replaced by a guyed mast standing 1,265ft (385m) in 1964 – an identical mast is still in use at Belmont in Lincolnshire – and it was this which made Emley known round the world.

The mast was made up of curved steel segments topped by a lattice section and finally a capping cylinder. The structure regularly became coated with ice in winter and icicles also formed on the guy ropes, adding to the strain. Falling ice was a threat to motorists on the several minor roads in the area and the mast was fitted with red warning lights to advise drivers of the danger.

The roads were closed on March 19 when packed ice began to fall from the tower but such was the weight of ice round the top of the mast – and the effect of the wind – that at one minute past five the entire mast crashed to earth, large chunks of it across Jagger Lane at its junction with Common Lane.

One falling cable sliced through a church, debris was scattered over a wide area and the noise of the collapse could be heard miles away but, remarkably, no-one was hurt. The boffins moved quickly; ITV signals were being received within four days and BBC2 coverage was back inside 48 hours.

An official inquiry reported that the collapse was due to the mast oscillating in a low-speed but steady wind. They recommended remedial work on the masts at Belmont and Winter Hill, including the hanging of 50 tons of steel chains within the structure, and both are still transmitting. Work began on building the new concrete tower at Emley Moor in 1969 and the first signals were received in Yorkshire homes on January 21, 1971. The structure was designed by Ove Arup and Partners and was designated a Grade II listed building "of significant architectural and historic interest"

The sun sets behind Emley Moor television mast.

in 2002. Reaching the Tower Room at the top of the concrete structure requires a seven-minute journey by lift to a height of 900ft (275m) and above that stretches the antenna which measures 184ft (56m).

Unfortunately, public access to the Tower Room is not available – imagine the view from up there on a clear day – but a car park on Jagger Lane, which connects the villages of Emley and Shelley off the B6116, offers a close-range view of the structure. **BB**

EMMERDALE FARM

Emmerdale (the Farm bit was dropped in 1989) seemed to have everything going for it when it was first broadcast on October 16, 1972. *The Archers* proved that we had an insatiable appetite for the humdrum doings of country folk and the world's longest-running radio soap never even set foot out of the studio. How could Ambridge, evoked by mooing noises and other rudimentary sound effects, compete with Beckindale which we could actually see nestling in beautiful Arncliffe in Littondale? This, after all, was the place that inspired Charles Kingsley to write *The Water Babies*. But, for some reason, the show's rural charms perennially failed to reach the sort of audiences chalked up by the urban top-raters like *Coronation Street*, *EastEnders* and *Brookside*. Then in 1993, a plotline involving a plane crash (conveniently killing off stalwart characters who had served their time) lifted *Emmerdale's* profile. Broadcasting the episode close to the anniversary of the Lockerbie disaster attracted controversy and made it a talking point. Location shooting had moved to Esholt and then to a purpose-built location near Harewood. This is a sealed village where only performers, technicians and the fan club (once a year) are allowed to tread. Plus the gardener, Alison Barrie, who will have put in 10 years this summer. In some respects it's a thankless task since this is a village where nothing much grows – all the top soil of the area was stripped away during the creation of the fake community. The soil is wretched and the rabbits eat everything that isn't railed off or netted. The stone-built houses look as if they would bring a smile to any estate agent's face if they came on the market. In fact, they have no value as residential properties. It was a condition of the original planning application that the buildings would have no

The Emmerdale TV village on the Harewood Estate.

The Replica of HM Bark Endeavour sails into Whitby Harbour.

life after *Emmerdale* and were built without proper foundations. There's no access or services either – all the water on site comes from a borehole – and the land must be restored as it was for agricultural use at the end of the show, if that ever happens. Strict security and a slightly surreal air characterise the place. There are no public tours and the once-popular public trips round the *Emmerdale* studio in Leeds were stopped when *Emmerdale* went six nights a week.
MH

ENDEAVOUR

For once the queue was worth it; an hour or so bent double in the cramped space of the crew's quarters, gazing in wonder from the deck at the complexity of the rigging and admiring the skill and fortitude of those who had sailed in all kinds of weather for three years brought *HM Bark Endeavour* to life in Whitby Harbour.

As one afflicted with a lifelong admiration for those who went to sea in sailing ships – beginning at the cinema with Charles Laughton as Captain Bligh and Robert Newton as Long John Silver, progressing through the *Hornblower* books to the tomes on Nelson – to actually stride aboard the replica of the ship James Cook took to Australia, New Zealand and back in an epic three year voyage spanning 1768–71 was to be in some kind of heaven.

For the pleasure of seeing just how tiny *Endeavour* was – and how small in stature the crew and scientist-passengers must have been, given the space they had in which to work, live and sleep – we have to thank the Australians, particularly Bruce Stannard, a journalist who had the initial idea of creating a new *Endeavour*, and Alan Bond, the America's Cup-winning skipper who provided the initial capital before his business empire collapsed and the Western Australian government, plus a few generous individuals, stepped in to finish the project.

Using documents from the National Maritime Museum at Greenwich, the Aussies were able to follow every specific of the original design, only varying the materials used when modern science offered improvements, in the making of the sails, for example.

Eight years after the keel was laid *Endeavour* was launched and two years later, on October 16, 1996, the vessel sailed from Fremantle on her first world voyage, including her first visit to Whitby.

It took her four years to return to Australia but in 2002 she headed for Cape Horn – making the passage in good weather, just as Cook had done in 1769 – and returned to Whitby on June 21, 2002. Using the North Yorkshire port as her base, she sailed along the Atlantic coastline from Spain to Norway before heading home from Whitehaven, arriving in Botany Bay on April 10, 2005.

Endeavour had sailed 170,000 nautical miles, visiting 29 countries and numerous Pacific islands and giving over 8,000 volunteers the opportunity of sampling life as an 18th century sailor.

Her work goes on – in 2007 she took part in the Australian Wooden Boat Festival – as do the efforts of marine archaeologists to find the remains of the original Endeavour. After being paid off by the Navy, the bark was renamed *Lord Sandwich* and used to carry troops across the Atlantic to fight the locals in the American War of Independence. She was scuttled in Newport Harbour to prevent a French fleet entering the Rhode Island port in support of the rebels. **BB**

ERIK BLOODAXE

Myth, legend or bloodthirsty reality, you wouldn't want to meet Erik Bloodaxe when he was having a bad day. This ruler of Northumbria and York for a few years in the 10th century had left home in Norway after, reputedly, killing most of his 20 brothers in order to succeed his father, Harald Finehair as king of western Norway.

Erik, variously described as brawny and awesome, had a reputation for taking whatever he fancied, his birthright being emboldened by marriage to the king of Denmark's daughter. For much insight to his life in Norway we have to rely on the folklore in the Viking sagas, compiled in the 12th and 13th centuries. In 935 Erik fled to the north of England and in 947 was installed as King of Northumbria, with his court in Jorvik, later York. Listen to how present day locals refer to their city as "Yaahk"and you can see that to make any sense at all, the place Erik knew must have been pronounced as one syllable, "Yaahvk" – the "vik" being half-swallowed and said as "vk".

In 948, the Saxons, led by King Eadred, expelled Erik and he went wandering and plundering overseas, returning to England in 952 when he reigned over Northumbria and York for another two years.

His days were numbered and in 954 Erik was killed in battle at Stainmore, County Durham, along with his son, brother, five Hebridean kings and two earls from Orkney – thus ending Scandinavian supreme power in the North. Viking raids resumed towards the end of the 10th century and their various incursions through the river valleys of eastern England, such as the Swale, left a legacy of descendants, of which this writer is one, and place names. These include names ending in thorpe (a farm) and by (a village), thus Ainthorpe and Easby, plus hundreds of more complicated derivations, such as

Vikings re-enactment at Kirkstall Festival.

Giggleswick and Scarborough.

In York today the Jorvik Centre in Coppergate gives a vivid idea of Viking life and smells. It was underneath a demolished sweet-makers in Coppergate 40 years ago that diggers found a wealth of domestic detritus which had survived remarkably intact because of waterlogged conditions. It was an archaeological gold mine which prompted the invention of a whole new set of investigatory techniques. It also revealed what a filthy bunch the Vikings were at home, living in their own muck and fishbones. If you want to go and see this recreated for yourself, don't forget one local pronunciation – Yaahvk Centre. **FM**

EXPLOSIONS

Fireworks came to Huddersfield in 1890 when James Greenhalgh founded the Standard company. Along with Lion Fireworks and Brock, Standard made Huddersfield the fireworks capital of Europe.

During the 1950s and 1960s the company was famous for its advertising jingle, "Light up the sky with Standard Fireworks". They employed more than 500 people across three Yorkshire sites, very happily by all accounts. One former worker said: "I miss the camaraderie, it was like Butlins."

Competition from the the place where fireworks were invented, China, undermined the business.

Standard went into receivership in 1998 and was forced to reinvent itself, repackaging and testing fireworks imported from its parent company in the Far East to ensure they meet British safety standards.

But remember, remember the reason for the bangs and the bonfire parties. It was a chap – in fact, several chaps – who came from round here who were responsible. In the archives of York Minster is a book containing the records of baptisms, marriages and funerals for the church across the road, St Michael-le-Belfrey. At some point in the book's history someone scored a deep pencilled cross next to a tiny entry.

You can make out in the scrawl of ecclesiastical Latin an F and then the name that is now one of the most infamous in England's history: Guy Fawkes. A hotel across the road from St Michael's claims to be his birthplace. More likely it was a building, now gone, which stood further back from the street and was accessed from an alley in Stonegate. Guy Fawkes planned something we are all too familiar with today – a terrible act of religiously-motivated terrorism – with his 12 fellow plotters choosing the day of the opening of Parliament to blow up the House of Lords.

They were Roman Catholics, bitter and angry men who lived at a time when their priests were hanged as traitors. Some believe the plot was a set-up and the conspirators naive men whose discovery in the nick of time would serve as an excuse for the fierce repression by the Protestant authorities which followed. Yorkshire, a Catholic hotbed, reeled. Three of the Gunpowder conspirators, Guy Fawkes and Jack and Kit Wright were former pupils of the now deeply establishment St Peter's public school in York.

The school's former headmaster had spent 20 years in prison for his faith. Guy Fawkes was tortured on the rack for days and the signature on his confessions was one word – "Guido". **MH**

York celebrating the 400th anniversary of Guy Fawkes and "gunpowder, treason and plot"

**Fell runners
pass Ribblehead
Viaduct.**

FIGURES IN A LANDSCAPE

Henry Moore

The undulating outlines of Henry Moore's monumental figures are best seen against a Yorkshire backdrop where he was born. Moore's work was what most people had in mind when terms like "modernism" and "abstract" were used – often jeeringly – as shorthand for pretentious. He was actually the most down-to-earth and practical of men, the seventh of Raymond Spencer Moore's eight children in Castleford. His father's job was mining engineer, later under-manager of the Wheldale colliery. He regarded education as the means of keeping his children out of the pit, and he feared that being a sculptor was too close to manual work. But his son, after soldiering in the war, stuck to his plan and became the first student of sculpture at Leeds School of Art, where they even built him his own studio. The Leeds connection remains today with the Henry Moore Institute in the city. It's funded by the Henry Moore Foundation at Perry Green, in Much Hadham, Hertfordshire where Moore and his wife Irina had moved in 1940. They lived fairly frugally, the exceptional wealth the artist accumulated being used to endow the foundation and help broaden the minds of those – if there are any left – who still sneer at modernism. **MH**

FISH AND CHIPS

Battered fish was probably a Jewish dish, originally brought in to London by immigrants from middle-Europe. We took to it at first bite and the original fast food survives despite the equally unhealthy in-roads made by chop suey and chicken curry, burgers and chicken thighs. Fish and chips is still the food you are most likely to see being eaten on the street, although people munching it on the hoof can appear crude and often create litter. If a "chippy" closes, the locality feels robbed. When this happened in our village, the butcher obligingly split his shop to make room for fish and chips. Once it was a cheap meal when North Sea fishing delivered apparently inexhaustible creels of white fish to market, now cod and haddock are expensive. A "fish supper" served in yesterday's papers, lined with a clean sheet of paper resilient to the heat and fats of the meal, has given way to a moulded tray. Beef dripping has mostly been succeeded by vegetable oil. Mushy peas (soaked and stewed dried peas) are still the side dish of choice, although maybe not with a curry-flavoured gravy. Choosing the country's best fish and chips shop is impossible. The most famous is easy. Harry Ramsden opened his first cafe in Bradford shortly after the 1914–18 war. In 1928 he opened a lock-up wooden shed not far away at Guiseley. His cooking methods were scientific: so many minutes in the fat, the use of stainless steel vats and buckets, and other quality controls that were rare. His shed grew to a restaurant, still with a take-away section and was famous for decades before becoming a world-wide franchise. In Whitby, the Magpie is renowned – and made national headlines because its queues annoy neighbouring businesses and the council. In Leeds, there is the celebrated Bryan's and the quaint restaurant founded by the Brett brothers not far from Headingley cricket ground and immortalised by one of its most passionate patrons, the late John Arlott. **FM**

Fish and chips – as served at the renowned Magpie in Whitby.

FLAG WAVING

Yorkshire Day

For almost 30 years, one of Yorkshire's great summer spectacles was the sight of Colin Holt marching resolutely around York's city walls with the media in tow. The tradition continues, but Holt died a year ago, aged 61. As founder and chairman of the Yorkshire Ridings Society, his message was simple and unchanging: that the sidelining of Yorkshire's ancient North, West and East Ridings, under local government re-organisation in 1974, was a crime and an insult. The society, founded in the wake of it campaigned "to protect the Yorkshire identity", make people more aware of the county's heritage and, more quixotically perhaps, restore the Ridings to their former importance. All of this was admirable but not necessarily attention-grabbing. Colin Holt's special talent was to grab attention. His first coup was to make his job as the society's publicity officer more challenging by putting himself out of reach by telephone at the cottage he shared with his wife Hilary at Fenwick, a small village north of Doncaster. The Holts refused to pay bills addressed to "Fenwick, South Yorkshire" rather than "Fenwick, West Riding". Eventually, after many official letters, British Telecom cut them off and the phone sat silent on their sideboard, gathering dust for several years. His second coup was

Henry Moore: The Castleford born artist became the first student of sculpture at Leeds School of Art

Yorkshire Day: A celebration of all things Yorkshire – every 1st August.

to devise Yorkshire Day, a celebration of all things Yorkshire, with the possible exception of whippets and ferrets. Every August 1, with white roses in their buttonholes, society members make a clockwise circuit of York's city walls. Pausing at the four "bars" or gates, they read out the Yorkshire Declaration of Integrity to an audience of radio and television reporters and slightly puzzled foreign tourists. The declaration, a specially-written statement of faith in the Yorkshireness of Yorkshire, is recited in four versions – Latin, Anglo-Saxon, Old Norse and modern English. Interest in Yorkshire Day has spiralled over the years. August 1 was chosen because it was on this day in 1759 that soldiers from Yorkshire regiments who had fought in the battle of Minden picked white roses as a tribute to fallen comrades.
GH

FLAT CAPS

(and whippets and ferrets)

Said to be typical of Yorkshire but no longer celebrated as such, even by those who strive to maintain the best traditions of the county (see below). By rights, there ought to be a steady demand for the flat cap which is still de rigueur for those who hang over the rail at livestock auction marts. But, of course, none of that headgear on show has been purchased in the last 25 years. The Yorkshire desire to stay ahead of the pack took a terrible knock six years ago with the closure of the JW Myers factory – the world's biggest cap maker – at Holbeck in Leeds. Its heyday was in the 1920s but after 111 years, production was switched to the Chinese city of Panyu. Kangol, the parent company of JW Myers, seems more interested in turning the heads of DJs and rappers who look daft

putting their caps on back-to-front. Kangol hope it's only a matter of time before stolid Yorkshire farmers attending agricultural shows follow this trend set by Grandmaster Flash and such-like and finally invest in new headgear. As the flat cap falls, the baseball cap rises, but that's a fashion icon that tells a different tale. Asda has just delivered some good news with sales figures showing flat caps up more than 80 per cent. Are they the correct dun colour with greasy brim? No, almost all the buyers are in the south-east where the most popular model is a country-style burgundy and brown number. **MH**

FLYING SCOTSMAN

and Yorkshire railways

Who can beat Yorkshire for railway heritage? We can boast the most glamorous, the oldest and the highest. Beginning with the oldest, the Middleton Railway harnessed horses to carriages in 1758 to carry coal from Middleton colliery along a rail track. As the oldest commercial rail operation in the world, it didn't intend to be left standing by rivals who were eyeing up the possibilities of new-fangled steam machinery and, in 1811, commissioned the first working steam locomotive. This got up sufficient momentum to drive an industry in Leeds for more than 150 years, a period when locos from the Hunslet Engine Company were exported all over the world. The Middleton line was going nowhere in the late 1950s, but it was restored in the 1960s by enthusiasts and reopened with volunteers operating passenger and freight services – another first. Recently they got hold of £737,500 from the Heritage Lottery Fund and have just opened a resource centre where the historic locos, including a newly-acquired Hunslet-built Brookes No 1, are on show. At the opening

Flat caps in all their infinite variety.

was Sir William McAlpine, former owner of the most glamorous engine in the country, probably the world. Originally numbered engine 1472 (soon altered to the celebrated 4472) the *Flying Scotsman* cost £7,944 when it steamed out of LNER's Doncaster works on February 7, 1923. LNER's chief mechanical engineer Nigel Gresley finessed the design so that it could do London to Edinburgh, 392 miles, non-stop on one tender of coal. In 1934 it achieved the first authenticated 100mph by a steam loco. LNER became the definitive railway brand – for a child the murmured repetition of the initials sounded like the rhythmic movement of a train over the sleepers.

A couple of years ago, engine 4472 was to be sold abroad until campaigners backed by Sir Richard Branson and the *Yorkshire Post* stepped in and acquired it for the National Railway Museum. It is currently laid up, undergoing a £700,000 overhaul to resolve long-standing mechanical problems which resulted in passengers aboard summer steam-drawn excursions from York to Scarborough being disappointed. They might have preferred a steam trip on Britain's highest railway, which also boasts further superlatives. The Settle-Carlisle was the last great mainline railway line to be constructed in Britain, the last to be built almost entirely by pick-and-shovel and, at Dent, it has the highest station in England. This recently opened as a holiday home with a kitchen which was once the ladies waiting room.

At Ribblehead station is a small visitor centre which tells the story of the 7,000 men who laboured for seven years to get this section and the famous Ribblehead viaduct open.

In 1869, St Leonard's church at Chapel-le-Dale had about 200 in its congregation. By 1871 nearly 1,000 navvies had been added to its flock as they laboured across some of the most inhospitable territory in the country.

Middleton railway as it is today.

Not that church-going was their strong-point. Today a few mounds are all that is left of their shanty towns. Although transience defined these forgotten workmen of the Victorian age, their struggles in a fierce landscape have a permanent memorial in the viaduct. **MH**

GANDHI

Ben Kingsley – born Krishna Bhanji – became Sir Ben in the New Year Honours of 2001 after his first big screen role, *Gandhi,* put his name permanently in lights. It won him the Oscar for best actor in 1983 and you could say he earned it by the sweat of his brow. The actor prepared by losing several stone and reading the 23 volumes of Gandhi's collected works. He comes from Snainton, although he grew up in Salford, where his Ugandan Asian father was a doctor and his mother, Anna, was an actress. It was seeing Ian Holm play Richard III that spurred his ambition, and his father advised that if he wanted to make it big, he would be better with an English name. It's a career that could have taken a different path. Brian Epstein once tried to add him to his Beatles portfolio after he had rocked the audience in a London musical. Trivia fans might cast their minds back to distant episodes of *Coronation Street*. Remember Ron Jenkins, who tangled with Ken Barlow's first wife Val? Sir Ben Kingsley, no less. **MH**

GAPING GILL

Are you ready for the drop? A steel bar locks into place across the lap and a retaining rope is threaded between the legs. There's a twinge of anxiety as your steel seat hanging from a cable on a scaffold wobbles slightly. The cable unwinds at 420 feet a minute from the winch and, as daylight rapidly disappears, there's a sense of dropping into limitless space.

The trip in the steel seat is brief and wet. A minute later, unclipped and peering up from the bottom, you are staring wondrously at a place big enough to accommodate the nave of York Minster. Welcome to Gaping Gill. A slender opaque plume of water vapour arcs elegantly through the one shaft of light from above. To the left, two cataracts crash thunderously down into the gloom past deeply fissured walls. This isn't exactly a journey to the centre of the earth, but first time round, Gaping Gill seems one of the wonders of the world. About an hour's signposted walk from Clapham near Settle brings you here. In 1842, farm labourers lowered John Birkbeck, a landowner and banker from Settle, on a rope to a ledge 190 feet down.

By 1895 Birkbeck's Ledge was still as far as anyone had descended Gaping Gill. As Yorkshiremen debated how to get down the remainder of the main shaft, a Frenchman called Edouard Martel came along and did it. The cavers' kit has changed since the thick tweed jackets of the Martel era and so have the techniques. Jumble sale woolies followed tweed clothing, then wetsuits and today the

Gaping Gill

preferred option is a French-made neoprene garment under a waterproof, one-piece suit.

They switched from those first lengths of hemp rope to ladders made with ash rungs and canal-hauling rope, then to aluminium ladders. Now they use hi-spec ropes for SRT – single rope technique – where the caver abseils to the bottom, then inches up the rope again like a frog. Halfway up to Gaping Gill you pass Ingleborough Cave, where the water from Fell Beck finally emerges into the daylight again. Discovered in 1837, Victorian ladies came to gaze at its stalagmites and other marvels, all now floodlit. Cavers do get a bit hot under the collar over criticism that they are all idiots who get themselves stuck and then require the emergency services to come and extract them. They point out that when things do occasionally go wrong underground, it's cavers who rescue cavers. **MH**

GINNEL

The word dates from the 13th century, a time when the people who ran the country spoke French, or a version of it. Ginnel comes from "venele" meaning alley (also derived from French). The Anglo-Normans had no knowledge of back-to-backs, but when these closely packed terraces of houses mushroomed in the 19th century in industrial Yorkshire and elsewhere, the ginnel got a new lease of life to describe the entry between properties to a shared yard at the rear. In a long terrace of houses, a ginnel was required to get you to the communal lavatory in time. In the West Midlands, they prefer "jennel", not quite the equivalent of twitchel – the name for a little path in the Nottingham area. **MH**

GLIDER

Sir George Cayley

The magnificent man in the flying machine is Sir Richard Branson. He was only up for a few seconds in a replica of a Cayley Flyer on the 150th anniversary of the first manned flight. The "father of aviation" Sir George Cayley had annoyed his wife by testing his first gliders on the staircase of their home at Brompton Hall. It tested marital harmony, but also helped him work out the basics of aerodynamics – weight, lift, drag and thrust – and to reach for the sky 50 years before Wilbur and Orville Wright. John Appleby was the world's first pilot in 1853, which must have made a change from his day job as Sir George's coachman. He had been "volunteered" by his boss and after farm workers on the end of ropes ran down a slope to get the contraption into the air, John Appleby flew it for 200 yards before crash landing. It was not a career he fancied, however. John is reputed to have said, "I was hired to drive, not to fly, " and promptly quit. **MH**

THE GOOD OLD DAYS

Leeds City Varieties

Let's do the time warp again. The good old days are not yours, or even your parents', but your great, great grandparents'. Why would you want to go there? Well, there's the building for a start and an auditorium which hasn't changed much since 1865 when it opened as Thornton's New Music Hall and Fashionable Lounge. In the late 1890s, it changed to City Palace Varieties and in its heyday, 2,000 people elbowed their way in to watch the likes of Marie Lloyd, Houdini and Charlie Chaplin in his pre-Hollywood years as one of the Lancashire Lads clog dancing troupe. They must have been pungent, raucous nights where no quarter was given for acts who failed to please. When the Second World War was over, the City Varieties looked round and discovered it was the oldest music hall in Britain still standing. Its performers, unfortunately, were all dead. Variety, on the other hand was very much alive and, in 1953, a BBC producer in Yeadon, Bernard (Barney) Colehan, spotted that the City Varieties' failure to adapt to the times was actually an asset. Colehan thought television needed brightening up (even if it was all black and white) and reckoned a bit of Edwardian effervescence and colour was just the ticket. So *The Good Old Days* was born and rollicked along for 30 years. The audience hammed it up under the chairmanship of Leonard Sachs, the archly grandiloquent chairman. The likes of Morecambe and Wise (fee 25 guineas) were happy to overlook the absence of star treatment back stage. None of the tiny, spartan dressing rooms had a shower and the washbasins weren't too clever either. The stage is smaller than many amateurs would think acceptable, there's only one way off and practically no wings. The stars put up with it for the huge television exposure. Colehan lured Eartha Kitt into *The Good Old Days* in 1972 with the promise that she could have Chaplin's dressing room. Later, a technician asked Colehan how he knew which one was Chaplin's? "I don't, " said Colehan. "And neither will she." Danny La Rue closed the final TV show on Christmas Eve 1983 with *We'll Meet Again* – not a music hall number but it fitted the mood. After a five year gap, they re-started *The Good Old Days* without the telly. They have had to adapt to reduced circumstances, but if they could bottle the atmosphere they generate at one of these evenings they'd have a supermarket winner. The Heritage Lottery Fund agreed in autumn 2007 to release the purse strings on the £9.2m needed to safeguard the old place's future. **MH**

Sir Richard Branson in a replica of Sir George Cayley's Flyer.

**The Great Yorkshire Show, where fashion meets farming.
Model Hollie Waugh cools off a Highland cow.**

GREAT YORKSHIRE SHOW

My first experience of the Great Yorkshire Show was fairly recent, 1991. Like many other East Riding born and bred lads, to travel across to Harrogate in the 1960s, '70s and '80s seemed a mighty long way, especially when we already had the fantastic Driffield Show (the largest one-day agricultural show) on our doorstep. I am also a Hull lad and the Hull Show, years ago, was one of the highlights of the year, along with Hull Fair week, when the country came to the city. But since 1991 I have never missed a Great Yorkshire and I feel very much a part of the family. I even came up with an event that has now become a regular part of the programme where we get housewives to choose their favourite cattle breed. For me, the cattle sheds, hives of activity as they prepare stock for show, and the bonhomie that exists around all of the livestock areas is what the show is all about. Turning up at the showground on the weekend prior to the show, as well as the night before, is a time to renew friendships. For me, it is that which means more than anything. The show lasts for three days. Tuesday is the big day for livestock when most farmers attend, but Wednesday is strong, too. Thursday is usually when those who are showing stock can relax and take time out to see all of the other wonderful sights including excellent show jumping and masses of other demonstrations. **CB**

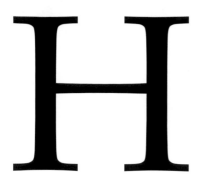

HARLOW CARR

Harlow Carr, Harrogate. Sounds a bit posh, but it's a spot anyone can visit, particularly if they like gardening. It was at Harlow Carr, or rather Harlow Hill, that, in 1950, the Northern Horticultural Society opened Harlow Carr Botanical Gardens. The NHS had been founded just four years earlier with the objective of "promoting and developing the science, art and practice of horticulture with special reference to the conditions pertaining to the north of England". Initially, the society leased 10.5 hectares of mixed woodland, pasture and arable land at Harlow Hill – an ancient royal hunting ground – from Harrogate Corporation. This has now been extended to almost 60 acres. They say that if a plant will grow at Harlow Carr, it will grow anywhere because the soil and the situation there at are not the friendliest. And things do grow at Harlow Carr, which is why thousands of people flock to the gardens every year to marvel at the trees, shrubs and flowers. And there's much more, including a restaurant, a plant centre and the chance to attend courses as varied as how to construct a hanging-basket, to how to learn about photographing plants. In 2001, the NHS merged with the Royal Horticultural Society, a getting-together which has seen a sea change in the gardens' development and management. Long may it continue. **DO**

HARVEY NICHOLS

When London fashion emporium Harvey Nichols announced that it was launching a first sister store somewhere in the provinces, more than a few perfectly tweezed eyebrows arched in quizzical haughtiness. When it was understood that the chosen venue was to be Leeds, right at the heart of "Oop North", there was much bemused bafflement, particularly among the capital's fashionistas, who at that time were a pack of middle-aged, chain-smoking gals who dressed in black and modelled themselves on Patsy in *Absolutely Fabulous*, Harvey Nicks' most famous fictional customer (actually, they haven't changed). "God, Edina, they'll be wearing Prada with their wellies on t'farm!" (Loud snorts followed by another swig of Bolly.) Some folk in Leeds also took a dim view, not least the city council's women's committee, which decided that promotional posters of model Jodie Marsh wearing a shocking pink dog collar and leash, with the witty slogan "Harvey Nichols Leeds (not follows)", were degrading and sexist. This caused the required stir and there were queues round the block when the five-storey glistening glass building finally opened its doors on October 19, 1996. The store became so crowded that at one point the escalators were stopped and the doors closed again. The official opening ceremony was performed by

Dita Von Teese performing at the tenth birthday celebration of Harvey Nichols in Leeds.

Canadian singer k d lang. HN Leeds has been a huge success ever since that day, the jewel in the crown of the Leeds's chicest shopping centre, the Victoria Quarter. The research had paid off – HN had picked Leeds over other possible contenders, such as the flashier Manchester and the more picturesque Edinburgh, because of its unusually wealthy catchment area. "A very high number of people within the 40–45 mile radius pay income tax at the higher rate, " said a spokesman at the time. Hot on the heels of the success of HN Leeds there are now more HN sister stores up and down the country, including ones in Manchester and Edinburgh, and there have been overseas openings too, in Riyadh, Dublin, Dubai and Hong Kong. Meanwhile, back in Leeds, Harvey Nichols continues to be at the hub of Yorkshire life, making sure its residents are not only well dressed but also well fed – it hosts the annual Yorkshire Post Taste Awards. Last October, for the store's 10th birthday, a massive bash was held in the Victoria Quarter, which saw burlesque artist (ie posh stripper) Dita Von Teese cavorting naked in a huge bubble-filled champagne glass (this time, no one asked why – not even the city council's women's committee). It's an institution. Whether buying, browsing or dining in the fabulous Fourth Floor Restaurant, Harvey Nichols Leeds is absolutely the place to be seen (though preferably not while wearing wellies with your Prada). **SS**

HAVE A GO

Wilfred Pickles and Mabel

His Yorkshire vowels crackled out of hulking wooden radio sets in homes across the country. "'Ow do, " said Wilfred Pickles, and "'ow are yer?" Pickles was a polymath: actor, producer, entertainer, news reader and lover of poetry (he edited several anthologies). He was also innovative, well ahead of his time. Between 1946, when the first of his programmes was broadcast from Bingley, and 1967, Pickles fronted *Have A Go* – the first give-away show on British radio, which at its zenith pulled in 20 million listeners and received 5,000 letters per week (one couple walked from Sheffield to Leeds to take part in it). The format was uncomplicated but, for the period, revolutionary. The public was invited to tell Pickles a story about themselves and could then win money – originally £1.17s.6d – in a quiz. The tone was always cosily warm, like a family gathering. Pickles's wife Mabel dispensed the cash – "Give 'em the money, Mabel" was another Pickles catchphrase – and Violet Carson, later to become the hair-netted Ena Sharples in *Coronation Street*, played the piano. There was a particular gusto about the audience sing-song of the programme's theme tune.

Have a go, Joe, come on and have a go
You can't lose owt, it costs you nowt

In its 21-year run, *Have A Go* clocked up almost half a million miles as it toured every corner of Britain and turned Pickles into a celebrity. He was viewed in BBC publicity terms as "The Common Man" and "Man of the People", and his regional bonhomie extended, during the War, to news reading. Each bulletin ended with the farewell: "... and to all in the North, good neet." He made film appearances in *Billy Liar*, starred in the TV series *For the Love of Ada* (with Irene Handl) and fronted *Stars on Sunday*. Born in Halifax in 1904, he died in Brighton – holding Mabel's hand – in 1978. A map of the West Riding permanently hung on the wall of his flat. **DH**

Wilfred and Mabel Pickles on the set at YTV.

HIGHEST POINT

Don't let anyone tell you otherwise, Whernside is not the highest point in Yorkshire. That honour falls to Mickle Fell, a lonely outpost of the Pennines, which, at 788m (2,585ft) is not only the highest point in the old county of Yorkshire (before it was ripped apart by boundary changes) but also the highest point in the administrative county of County Durham. Mickle Fell lies in the middle of a boggy moor miles from anywhere, but its distinctive outline can be seen from many of the Lake District hills. And for those who love bits of useless information, Mickle Fell is a Marilyn – a mountain or hill in the British Isles separated from its neighbours by a height of at least 150m. The name Marilyn was coined as a humorous contrast to Munro, used to define

a Scottish mountain with a height of more than 3,000 ft. If we have to have Whernside as our official high point, it stands at 736m, and stares across the valley to the second highest hill, Ingleborough, which at 723m is some 27m higher than the third of Yorkshire's famous Three Peaks, Penyghent.
DO

HIGHWAYMAN (DICK TURPIN)

Pock-marked, brutal, sadistic – it's strange how history throws up folk heroes who most of us, if we met them today, would gladly see put away. A sentimental Victorian ballad even sang of "Brave Turpin hero bold". It's the horse really that made Dick's name, although the ride from London to York on Black Bess never happened. Turpin was an

Essex boy, an apprentice butcher, who went to ground after a life of lucrative gangsterism on his home turf, not on the Costa de Sol, but in East Yorkshire. He called himself John Palmer but his true identity was revealed after a typical incident of thuggery when he shot a rooster belonging to the landlord of the Ferry Inn in Brough. In 1739 Turpin was hanged at Tyburn on York's Knavesmire. **MH**

MR AND MRS HOCKNEY

No parents have ever figured so prominently in an artist's work than Kenneth and Laura Hockney. But then it was his mother and father's example and solid support – practical, emotional and financial – which enabled David Hockney to burst out of Bradford and become an artist in the first place. The Hockney household was a strict but loving and tolerant place. Kenneth and Laura embraced individuality, however unconventionally conveyed, and didn't mind the paint that was frequently spilt on the bedroom carpet. Kenneth was fiercely political (devout in his campaigning for CND), a conscientious objector during the Second World War, a devotee of the arts and an amateur painter (attending Bradford School of Art) and always fastidiously smart in attire. "He taught me not to care what the neighbours think, " said Hockney admiringly. Laura was teetotal, vegetarian and staunchly Methodist. Asked to name someone he considered beautiful, Hockney replied proudly: "My mum". A painting of Kenneth – one of his initial experiments with oils – was the first painting Hockney sold. The buyer paid £10 for it at the biennial Yorkshire Artists Exhibition in Leeds in 1955. Kenneth had bought the original blank canvas, set up the easel for his son, sat for the portrait and made sure the mirror was arranged in such a way that he could study

its progress . "I've sold my dad, " Hockney told his mother. Laura became a regular subject over more than 40 years; Hockney caught her in ink, paint and also in a 1982 photocollage among the ruins of Bolton Abbey. He drew her on the day of his father's funeral in 1978 and on her deathbed in Bridlington 21 years later. His fascination with – and fondness for – for his parents is emphasised in *My Parents* (1977), a minimalist but vividly striking double portrait in which Laura, grey-haired and bright-eyed, with her hands folded on her lap, stares directly out of the painting and Kenneth, immaculately neat, is distracted in a book: Aaron Scharf's *Art and Photography*. Caught in the mirror is a postcard of della Francesca's *The Baptism of Christ* to illustrate his parents' Christian values. On the bottom shelf is a book about Chardin – an 18th century French artist who dwelt on domestic affairs – and Proust's *Remembrance of Things Past*. If questioned about why he painted his parents so often, Hockney explained very simply: "It's my way of communicating with them." **DH**

HOLBECK HALL HOTEL

Getting swiftly down from the hotel to the beach at Scarborough in June is what we'd all like to do. Unfortunately in 1993 it was the hotel which was making its way to the sea. The Holbeck Hall hotel slid down the South Bay cliffs without warning in one of Britain's biggest-ever landslides. As it began to collapse into the abyss, it became for a brief time one of the resort's star attractions. Television pictures were beamed around the world and Alison Graham reported for the *Yorkshire Post* on the biggest free show in town: *After bleak, wet days the sun finally burst out to illuminate the resort's most unorthodox and unexpected tourist attraction, the ruined*

Holbeck Hall Hotel, Scarborough.

Holbeck Hall Hotel. Crowds came in their droves. There were hundreds of them... Here was a very different type of sightseer. This was middle England in car coats. The hard core was elderly, well-dressed couples who turned a tiny park overlooking the disaster zone into a sea of prosperous, crisp polyester. Clutching Sunday newspapers they dozed, they pointed and they poured out flasks of tepid Nescafe into plastic cups while removing immaculate sandwiches from clingfilm... Many were making repeat visits. One old man, shrouded in a miasma of sweet-smelling pipe smoke told anyone who would listen: "We were there when the veranda went. It was terrible, terrible." This was a piece of history which anyone could watch. And age was no barrier to stealthy and determined efforts to get close to the wreckage. They dipped under 'Police – No entry' tapes and skirted fences to teeter precariously on ledges... Toddlers well-covered against the piercing sunlight lurched from the anxious grasps of parents who had become born-again civil engineering experts. "The roof's going to go next. Then the whole lot's definitely going to go.

Definitely." A breezy paperseller in a blue overall stood amid piles of the Scarborough Evening News. "These are special editions, they are souvenirs, " he yelled. "In a few years' time they'll be worth double the price." As they cost 25p, it hardly seemed a gilt-edged investment. This was the most blatant example of the entrepreneurial spirit. Muriel's Quality Ices van was doing a brisk trade. But there was nothing else. And anything more would have been unseemly in the genteel surroundings of the South Cliffe. The Holbeck Hall Hotel itself was an eerie, half-eaten corpse of a building perched at the top of a gash in the cliffs, a monstrous broken wound weeping tons of debris. Its welcoming sign – "gardens overlook the South Bay" – took on a strange poignancy. Dining tables and crockery lay where they fell, looking for all the world like an abandoned picnic on the Gaza Strip. On blackboards advertising pleasure boat cruises around the bay the words 'Trips to Fawlty Towers' were crudely chalked. Just over a year later, the owners of Holbeck Hall, Barry and Joan Turner, were offered a deal by the insurers to find a suitable alternative hotel and be given the money to purchase it. They bought Charingworth Manor in the Cotswolds for around £2.25m. It's about 40 miles from the sea. **MH**

HOLE OF HORCUM

It was scooped out by the Devil for his punchbowl, according to legend. The more prosaic truth is that this considerable hollow, a full mile across, which surprises and intrigues drivers along the road out of Pickering heading for Whitby, was caused by springs. The Hole's fascination remains undimmed and paths along its floor and round its rim form a popular circuit. The last steps of the walk are often over the threshold of the adjoining roadside Saltersgate Inn where in the winter the welcoming blaze in

the cadaverous ancient fireplace is a wonderful restorative. The pub, on the fringe of the mysterious moors, used to be where smugglers traded. They brought salt up from Whitby in panniers with contraband hidden beneath. A Customs man, who caught them red-handed at the pub, got beaten to death and his body buried under the hearth. To discourage further enquiries, the culprits invented a story about the Devil coming to terrorise the neighbourhood if the fire is allowed to go out. **MH**

HUMBER BRIDGE

From time immemorial, ferries took people across the Humber estuary between Hull and Barton. In 1966 a Labour government was hanging on to power by its fingertips with an overall majority of two. They could not afford to lose a by-election at North Hull and even Prime Minister Harold Wilson came to town to campaign. One of the other Labour big guns who arrived was Barbara Castle, the Minister for Transport. She said if the locals voted in the Labour candidate, they could have a Humber Bridge. When opened by the Queen in July 1981, its 2,220m (7,283 ft) length made it the world's longest single-span suspension bridge. Although it has since been overtaken by three others, the bridge was ranked sixth in the seven wonders of Britain in a recent poll of travellers. This leaves the question of the bill. The original estimate of £28m grew to £98m and by the time the Queen came it had shot up to £151m. It kept skyrocketing and quite a bit is still owing – £334,436,987 according to the most recent Parliamentary answer last year – and it won't be paid off until 2038. **MH**

The Humber Bridge

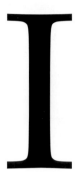

ICEBERG

and Wallace Hartley

The hold that the *Titanic* still has over the public mind can be judged from the fact that only a couple of months ago a service was held in Southampton to commemorate the sinking of theWhite Star liner which went down in the early hours of April 15, 1912, with the loss of 1,523 lives. Titanic , thought to be unsinkable, had sailed from Southampton on April 10 for New York via Cherbourg and Cobh in Ireland. As the stricken vessel prepared to slip under the icy North Atlantic waters, the bandmaster, a violinist called Wallace Hartley whose home was in Dewsbury, ordered the band to play on. Many of the survivors claimed that Hartley and his band kept going till the very end, but none of the performers survived to confirm it. Some survivors remembered hearing the hymn *Nearer, My God, to Thee*. Former colleagues recalled that Hartley had told them he would play either that, or *O God, Our Help in Ages Past* if he was ever on a sinking ship. Titanic 's wireless officer, Harold Bride, thought he had heard them performing a hymn called *Autumn* or a popular song of 1912 called *Songe d'Automne*. Wallace Hartley's body was recovered from the water numbered as body 224. But his final act had struck an immediate chord with the public – 1,000 people came to his funeral and 40,000 lined the route of his funeral procession. A blue plaque marks his house in Dewsbury. **MH**

ICE CREAM

Alexander the Great wouldn't fight without it, Nero wouldn't contemplate an orgy without it, and a day at the seaside just wouldn't be right without it. Ice cream's role in history is welldocumented.

The living proof that the qualities that made Alexander and Nero such fans of early forms of the stuff is there to be seen on any day – sunny or otherwise – on the Yorkshire coast. There isn't a better place to enjoy an ice cream than Scarborough or Bridlington. It goes with the sea air as naturally as fish and chips, especially in a handful of remaining ice-cream parlours that serve it with a delicious whiff of nostalgia for a more innocent age. Time was that virtually every town and city in Yorkshire had somewhere with a long counter stacked with the tall and tapering knickerbocker glory glasses and someone behind it who knew exactly how to pile in the layers of ice cream and top them

A poster advertising the White Star Line's ocean liner *Titanic*.

ICON: HANNAH HAUXWELL

The first the outside world knew about this lady farmer (who was contentedly making £3 a week) was when Yorkshire Post correspondent Alec Donaldson strolled into her farmyard early in 1970. She lived at Low Birk Hat Farm about 1,000 feet above sea level, where her parents had brought her when she was three. At the age of 34, she found herself working the farm's sour acres alone, living an isolated rural existence which was more typical of a Thomas Hardy novel than Seventies Britain. Television journalists followed in Donaldson's footsteps and, following the broadcast of Yorkshire Television's *Too Long a Winter* in 1973, the Lonely Lady of Birk Hat became a reticent worldwide celebrity. She left her spartan farmhouse on the edge of the Blackton reservoir in Teesdale 18 years ago and now, aged 80, lives on her own in a modest semidetached cottage in Cotherstone, a village less than five miles away from Birk Hat, just inside County Durham. Of her previous life, she says: "I existed during winter and truly lived during the summer. People always think that I was happy there, but it was not always the best of times. I was not always the happiest person in the world. I muddled on and I didn't rely too much on possessions; I cut my cloth according to my needs. But I think I showed a different slant on life, and that's what captured people's imaginations. These days there seems to be such a reliance on material things; it's all about keeping up with Joneses. I do not blame or begrudge people if they want nice things, but these things are not always what they really want. I have often said I was, still am, and always will be a plain country woman, and proud to be a plain country woman." **GH**

off with a cherry before handing over the long-handled spoon needed to get the last drop out of the bottom. But that was then, and now such palaces of pleasure are a rarity, and we should all treasure those that remain. There's only one left in Bridlington, and that's Tophams, on Cross Street, where it's possible still to while away the time over a sundae and watch the crowds wandering towards the harbour.

Scarborough has two, both on the seafront and both retro delights – Paccito's, with its bright red wicker chairs, and the Harbour Bar, with its expanse of bright yellow counter, its mirrors, and the vintage signs saying things like "Get Your Vitamins the Easy Way – Eat Ice Cream Every Day". Nero would have approved. **AV**

Gareth Gates: Once the most famous teenager in Britain.

IDOL: GARETH GATES

We all remember Gareth Gates. He was a likeable spiky-haired youngster with a big musical talent. The boy who had, by the age of 11, been head chorister at Bradford Cathedral where he sang solo for the Queen, was also a pianist, classical guitar player and student at the Royal Northern College of Music. He came into the nation's homes through the first *Pop Idol* in 2002 where he narrowly lost to Will Young. However, audiences had been captivated not only by his singing but also by his determination to overcome a lifelong stutter. When the contest was over, the runner-up got a recorddeal anyway from Simon Cowell and had the satisfaction of seeing his debut single,

Country life: Hannah Hauxwell drawing her water for domestic use at her farm in Baldersdale, early 1980s. Mike Cowling.

Unchained Melody , at the top of the UK charts, beating Will Young's first record. A string of hits followed and at 17, Gareth Gates had the world at his feet. Smash Hits magazine organised an International Gareth Day. He was the fastest-selling British artist ever and the most famous teenager in Britain. But the squeaky-clean image was tarnished by the much older pin-up Jordan. In a kissand- tell interview, she talked about her three-month affair with Gareth while she was pregnant. Aged 22, he tried to start again a few months ago with a new album, *Pictures Of The Other Side*. His new single, *Changes*, suggesting a more sombre musical direction, rose to number 14 in the charts and then stopped. But he has still shifted a total of 3.5 million singles and albums in this country alone. **MH**

INDEPENDENT

Yorkshiremen are immensely proud of their county. This self-regard reached its apogee when, half a lifetime ago, only those born in the county could play for its cricket team. This independent nature, or character, is arguably being eroded, lost if you will. Michael Vaughan is too mild and nice to be compared with the forthright (Sir) Geoffrey Boycott, a man so often right and so blunt with it. Fred Trueman was another man of his time; Harvey Smith matched him for square-jawed rebellion against the privilege-rich arena they worked in. David Hockney is not only a great portrayer of our landscape, giving life to the quiet wolds, but has put the proverbial two fingers up to the ban, in places, of smoking outside. Dickie Bird, Michael Parkinson, Alan Bennett are Yorkshiremen and proud enough never to hide it. Sir Jimmy Savile gets a special thank you for his accessibility for a quote, always returning a call. I suppose this independent,

larger-than-life thing has much to do with the fact that Yorkshire is Britain's largest county. It is a boast we have to carry, often with not enough humility. As only half a Yorkshireman (and only since the Danish invasion), I can sit in judgment on the fence, metaphorically and genealogically. It is, for example, obvious to anyone except the dismally bereft of intellect, that Yorkshire is immensely superior to Cheshire and similar effete counties, but is it better than Lancashire, Cumbria, Cornwall, Northumberland? To the foreigner our county is known for one small terrier and one large one, a dire song and a savoury batter pudding which hardly anyone can make properly.Where is our Lancashire hotpot or our Cornish Pasty?

The Yorkshireman does have one notable ability: this is informing us that he is a Yorkshireman. **FM**

INUNDATIONS

Great Yorkshire floods

It was on June 19, 2005 that flash floods washed cars into gardens and buildings collapsed in North Yorkshire, with Helmsley at the centre of the storm, and pretty little Hawnby was cut off. Drivers had to abandon their cars and climb trees to escape the rising waters of the River Rye. These extreme weather events are now becoming a regular pattern. It was just coming into February fill-dike when the worst flooding devastated Yorkshire in 1953, as the North Sea smashed against the East Coast with catastrophic results. Gales had been blowing for three or four days when the last Saturday in January dawned in Scarborough.What no-one on-shore realised was the severity of the storm the winds were blowing up. Hundreds of miles, away to the southwest of Iceland, an unusual surge in the sea had begun around midday on Thursday. Astrong anticyclone west of Ireland turned the storm south and as it entered the North Sea, the low pressure caused the sea level to bulge. High winds were driving the water outwards at the point where the coasts of eastern England and the Netherlands start to funnel together and where the sea becomes shallower. The combined effect was to intensify the wall of water heading for the shores. By midmorning at Scarborough, it was clear the sea had turned especially ugly. The Harbour Master, Captain JWK Hall, said later: "We knew shortly after 10 o' clock that something was wrong." Before serious danger arrived, there was time to relay warnings down the coast from north to south. But none were sent. By 6pm, the surge had reached the Wash and was causing damage. This stretch of coast was the responsibility of the Lincolnshire River Board which did not pass to the adjacent Essex River Board the news that terrifying sea conditions were heading their way. Some of these boards (which came under the Ministry of Agriculture) on the South-East coast had an arrangement for passing on information like this. But no similar system applied in the North. The Met Office had put out a weather warning, but this was long before local radio and 24-hour TV news. As the tide rose, water levels reached heights not seen in the previous 250 years. On the Lincolnshire coast, the main street of Sutton-on-Sea was suddenly eight feet under water. Sea defences were breached in 1,200 places and, as night turned to ghastly day, 307 people were found to have perished in the water. Evacuation plans were found seriously wanting and 22,000 people were made homeless between Lincolnshire and the Thames estuary. The answer was to build sea walls to keep similar chaos at bay. Not any more – now we bow to the fact that not all flooding is preventable and that protection can only be relative. Mark Tinnion, regional flood risk manager for the Environment Agency says today it's all about flood risk management. The owners of 260,000- plus properties are judged to be at risk from flooding in Mark's patch. The price of guaranteeing they will never get their feet wet is beyond our means. Even so, the Environment Agency is spending £413m on flood management in this financial year. All spending decisions are based on cost benefit – how many people it will affect, how much impact it will have on the environment. **MH**

IONICUS

His real name was Joshua Armitage and he contributed cartoons and drawings for Punch for more than 40 years. He learned serious drawing at Liverpool College of Art and served on minesweepers during the war. But his eyesight was poor and the Royal Navy found more suitable employment for him as a signals instructor, where there was time to contribute to the Admiralty-sponsored monthly magazine *Ditty Box – "the Navy's Own Magazine"*. The first cartoon Armitage got into Punch showed Ionic columns in the background and that gave him an idea for a penname – Ionicus. His gentle sense of humour and unique style won him many admirers, especially for his depictions of Bertie Wooster and his butler Jeeves on 58 of the covers of the Penguin PG Wodehouse paperback series. When Ionicus was commissioned by *Punch* to illustrate an article on Yorkshire caving, he began walking up Ingleborough in mist and rain looking for sketchable features. Bedraggled, he gave up the search and was directed to the office of *The Dalesman* – which in those days was the sitting room of a double-fronted house at Clapham lagged with books and files, including photographs taken in caves.

East coast floods, Mablethorpe February, 1953.

Ionicus, gratified for the loan of several pictures, agreed to produce a cover picture for the magazine. It was the start of a 16-year association with the magazine. **MH**

I SAY, JEEVES

August 14, 1913: PG Wodehouse is lolling in a deckchair on the boundary edge of Gloucestershire's sumptuous Cheltenham ground. A 25 year-old fastmedium bowler, Percy Jeeves – a Yorkshireman playing for Warwickshire – toils in the sun (0–43 in the first innings; 1–12 in the second). Gloucestershire beat Warwickshire by 267 runs and the statistical minutiae of the Championship game is absorbed into *Wisden's* vast dusty archives. But the literary consequences of it live on. For Wodehouse never forgot the bowler who caught his eye with a whippy action. In 1916, he published *The Man with Two Left Feet* – the first book to feature the dimwitted Bertie Wooster and his urbane and highly clever servant Jeeves. "I suppose," Wodehouse wrote many years later, "the name stuck in my mind." When the book appeared, the man whose identity Wodehouse borrowed for his comic creation had already died. Joining the Royal Warwickshire Regiment at the outbreak of War, Jeeves was killed during the Battle of the Somme on July 22 that same year. Born in Earlsheaton, near Dewsbury in 1888, he played for Goole CC and Hawes CC. He was unsuccessfully trialled by Yorkshire in 1910, but moved to Edgbaston two years later. In 50 appearances for Warwickshire he took 199 wickets at 20.03 and scored 1,204 runs. After his performance in the annual Gentleman v Players match at The Oval (4–44), Pelham Warner declared Jeeves would be a Test cricketer. War broke out a month later. **DH**

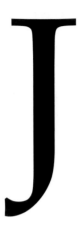

JAM AND JERUSALEM

Calendar Girls

Presentation, they say, is everything and it was a man, Terry Logan, who was the making of the *Calendar Girls*. It was Terry, a former ad man and watercolour painter, who composed the photographs for the 1999 calendar which immortalised the nude ladies of Rylstone and District Women's Institute, one of whom was his wife Lynda. Images that might easily have been cringe-making, cheesy and forgettable (like so many of the subsequent imitators) turned out to be brilliantly original and struck a profound chord. It all began when a bunch of friends of Angela Knowles, whose first husband, John Baker, had died of non-Hodgkin's lymphoma in July 1998, were wondering what might serve as a memorial for him. They reckoned that producing and selling a calendar that was a bit different might raise some cash for Leukaemia Research – if the *Yorkshire Post* could be persuaded to give the launch of it a few column inches. The newspaper obliged, and so did almost every other media organisation in the world. Their story became a Hollywood movie hit and now the few quid they originally hoped to raise is heading for the £1.5m mark. **MH**

JASON (AMY JOHNSON)

The original Jason was a mythical Greek, a dispossessed prince, who set sail with a trusty band called the Argonauts in search of a magical ram's fleece. Only if the golden fleece was recovered could Jason reclaim his father's kingdom from a usurper. The sea also played a part in the making of the woman adventurer involved with a modern-day Jason. Amy Johnson's father, John, owned a fish processing factory in Hull. But it was to be the sky rather than the water which exerted a pull she could not resist. After graduating from Sheffield University with a degree in Economics, she took up flying to keep the tedium of secretarial work at bay and passed her pilot's licence in July 1929. Unable to make a living from it, she became the first woman in the country to qualify as an Air Ministry ground engineer. Family and friends were talked into sharing the cost of buying an aeroplane, a £600 De Haviland Moth, named *Jason* after the family fish business. The aim was to break the world record for flying from the UK to Australia. Amy took off on May 5, 1930 from Croydon Aerodrome with only her father and a few others turning up to wave her off. By the time she had reached her first stop, Karachi, she was a worldwide celebrity. After 19 days, Amy touched down in Darwin on Saturday May 24, the first woman to fly solo to Australia. Once back in London she was driven through the streets in a open topped car with an estimated crowd of a million people lining the route and from there she flew home to Hull in a newly-repaired *Jason*. The following year she married a fellow-flier, Jim Mollison, and the flying exploits continued, both on her own and with her husband. The pair of them crashed attempting a non-stop flight east to west across the Atlantic and so did the marriage. When war came, Amy joined the Air Transport Auxiliary, flying aircraft from factory production-lines to RAF airbases.

On January 5 1941, she took off in freezing fog from Blackpool to deliver an aeroplane to an RAF base in Kidlington, Oxfordshire. Four and a half hours later she came down, miles off course, in the Thames Estuary. A seafarer, who saw her plane crash, died attempting a rescue. Amy's body was never found. **MH**

JET (WHITBY)

The beautiful soft texture, dense black colour and polish of Whitby jet has always been desirable. Jet beads have often been found in the burial places of bronze-age people and jet objects are often found in digs on Roman sites. In accounts at Whitby Abbey for the year 1394, a payment is recorded of seven pence for seven jet rings made by Robert Carr. He was the first to be known by name among the many locals engaged in the various activities of wrenching jet from the cliffs, hand-carving and polishing it. It was not only desired for decoration. Rubbing the jet causes a hint of smoke which was supposed to break spells or drive away devils. But it was Queen Victoria who made the shiny black gemstone a "must-have" for her many mourning costumes after the death of her beloved Prince Albert in 1861. Some

will claim today the real McCoy can only be found on seven miles of Yorkshire coast. In fact, jet has been worked throughout the northern half of the North York Moors. Farndale has numerous old jet drift mines and so does Rosedale. Thanks to the demands of the Victorian fashionistas who wanted to look like the Queen, in 1871 there were more than 20 jet workings in Bilsdale alone. For some places, it was like a mini-Gold Rush. The village of Great Broughton, forgotten since medieval times, sprang back to life when jet miners arrived and the village pub, the Jet Miners, was where mine owners bartered prices with manufacturers from Whitby. The boom did not long survive the death of Queen Victoria. An old jet workshop, abandoned in the 1950s in Burns Yard, off Flowergate, was shifted to the foot of the 199 Steps, where it now houses the Whitby Jet Heritage Centre. **GH**

JETS (RAF)

The huge runway at RAF Finningley (now under new management as Robin Hood airport) is where our last operational jet bombers used to touch down. Photos of the potent four-engined V-force, the Vulcan, Victor and Valiant, used to adorn the bedroom walls of many schoolboys in the late Fifties and early Sixties. They served the need for aircraft that could deliver a 10,000lb nuclear bomb from 45,000ft, on a target 3,500 miles away. It was the majestic Avro Vulcan which won the hearts of most fans in short trousers because the radical delta wing gave it such a glamorous look. The 1.92 miles long runway at Elvington Air Museum (ex- RAF again) can also accommodate these giants and the 2007 Yorkshire Air Show was billed as the noisiest in Elvington's history with the return of the mighty Vulcan to flight, with a Victor alongside. **GH**

A Victor 'V' Bomber which was one of the aircraft equipped to carry the 400 kt Thermo-Nuclear Bomb on show at the Elvington Air Museum, York.

JIM'LL FIX IT

Now then, now then. "Dear Jim, can you fix it for me to ... smoke a big fat cigar, wear loads of heavy jewellery and a lovely bright track suit, sit in a big seat and hand out special badges?" The theme tune that introduced the BBC's *Jim'll Fix It* – usually between *Dr Who* and *The Generation Game* was heard on Saturday nights from the mid-1970s. Each year 350,000 children wrote in, asking for Jimmy Savile to fix them things like the opportunity to drive a Lotus on a James Bond film set or press the button to demolish a chimney stack. It was better than working down a Leeds coal mine where he had started out and Jim kept at it for 20 series. Now aged 80, he could not resist when opportunity came knocking again in 2007 with an offer from UKTV Gold to present *Jim'll Fix It: Now and Then*, where adults who featured on the original show revisited their "fix-its". **GH**

STEPHEN JOSEPH

and Alan Ayckbourn

There are two large debts of thanks we owe Stephen Joseph. He proved that seaside theatre could be much more than end-of-the-pier shows and he gave a start to the playwright whose work is now produced more regularly than Shakespeare's. Stephen Joseph was the son of the actress Hermione Gingold and the publisher Michael Joseph. In America he was so inspired by seeing theatre in the round – instead of through a proscenium arch – that he decided to import the concept to the unlikely setting of Scarborough's public library. A hopeful 17-year-old got in touch about acting there, saying he had written a little at school. Joseph gave him a job and half a century and

70 plays on, Alan Ayckbourn is now artistic director of the theatre carrying Stephen Joseph's name. **MH**

JOWETT CARS

The car in front used to be a Jowett. Benjamin and William built their first one just over a century ago and the Jowett became the only mass-produced car to come out of Yorkshire. In Austerity Britain, most people's idea of motoring was trundling about in a patched-up family runabout, either built or designed before the war. But the Jowett Javelin, designed by Gerald Palmer, was all-new in 1946 and three victories at Le Mans for their sporty Jupiter model made them the wheels people wanted. The products that rolled out of Jowett's Springfield Works in Bradford Road, Idle, in West Yorkshire, ranged from reliable and economical vehicles, whose reputation made them the Volvos of their day, to hot little racers which could leave a Jaguar XK 120 standing at the traffic lights.

Their Jowett R4 used the, at the time, revolutionary laminated glass fibre for the body and had the first aircraft-style seats. This was a proud, trail-blazing company which seemed equipped to change lanes as engineering, taste or fashion indicated. Their day-to-day cars were trusted and robust. Their sports cars were sexy and beat the pants off the opposition. They couldn't go wrong, but they did. The company ceased trading in 1954. It was a case study in what had gone awry in a long list of things, from motorbikes to ships to knives and forks, that bore the title "Made in Britain". Jowett's chief test driver still describes it as a tragedy. **MH**

The Jowett Jupiter.

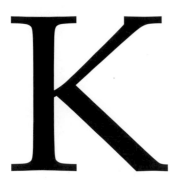

KICK OFF (SHEFFIELD FC)

Sepp Blatter, the president of Fifa, and Michel Platini, the president of Uefa, will both sit down at Sheffield FC's 150th anniversary dinner at the Cutlers' Hall this autumn, along with the Sports Minister and maybe even the Prime Minister.

The team, which plays in the heady heights of the UniBond League, is one of two to have received the Order of Merit from Fifa. The other is Real Madrid. How does such a lowly club mix in such exalted company? Simple: they are the oldest football club in existence, having been formed on October 24 1857, and their members invented the rules. Football had developed from the "anything goes" mayhem of the Middle Ages into a more codified sport and Sheffield's interpretation was the one that was followed. Two Old Harrovians, Nathanial Creswick and William Prest, are credited with forming the club, two years after members of Sheffield Cricket Club had begun to amuse themselves in the off-season by arranging informal kick-abouts.

In the beginning, Sheffield had to manufacture matches among their own members – marrieds versus singles being one – but the formation of the neighbouring Hallam club in 1860 provided the first official opposition, and the two clubs still meet every year. Sheffield was one of the first hotbeds of football and by 1862 there were 15 clubs in the city, all playing to Sheffield rules which were adopted by the Sheffield Football Association when it came into being in 1867.

Sheffield FC were by now looking outside the city for matches to provide them with competition and in March 1866 played a match against a London XI at Battersea. The club had joined the FA in 1863, but it was not until 1878 that they agreed to play to FA rules and within a few years they had begun to fade as an influence on the club game at the highest level as professionalism began to make inroads.

Heavy defeats at the hands of the professionals of Aston Villa, Nottingham Forest and Notts County signalled the days of the amateur were over, but Sheffield suggested to the FA that they inaugurate a knockout competition purely for the amateur game. This later became the FA Amateur Cup and was won by Sheffield in 1904. Over the past 150 years Sheffield have played on a number of grounds, starting at Bramall Lane and including spells at the Owlerton and Don Valley Stadiums, but never owned their own headquarters until they bought land adjacent to the Coach and Horses public house in Dronfield. A membership drive has recently netted England (cricket) captain Michael Vaughan. **BB**

The White Horse at Kilburn.

KILBURN WHITE HORSE

The largest and most northerly of England's white horses, the Kilburn figure, covering just over an acre of Roulston Scar not far from Sutton Bank, is 150 years old this year. Created by schoolmaster John Hodgson and his pupils, the horse was based on a drawing by artist Harrison Weir and paid for by Thomas Taylor, a businessman who travelled extensively and was inspired to finance the project after seeing similar figures in the south of the country. The horse fell into disrepair after the First World War but a public appeal launched by the *Yorkshire Evening Post* in 1925 raised the money to have it restored, and the landmark remained visible from across the Vale of York until it was covered in 1939 so it could not be useful to enemy aircraft. After being uncovered and whitened in 1946, the horse suffered badly when hit by a storm three years later and Robert Thompson, the famous furniture maker from Kilburn – who decorated his work with a trademark mouse – was among those who helped to restore the horse again. Now the KilburnWhite Horse Association, a charity, raises funds to maintain the horse, an on-going project fraught with difficulty given the size of the site and its position on a steep, unstable surface. The future of Kilburn's famous landmark seems secure. **BB**

KILNSEY CRAG

Cut by one of those glaciers which did so much to shape the Dales, Kilnsey Crag has for years been a source of disappointment, verging on depression. Its unique shape and position, seemingly hanging over the B6160 connecting Grassington and Kettlewell have made it one of the best-known landmarks in the country, the equal of Malham Cove and Gordale Scar in any Yorkshireman's catalogue of Dales gems.

The taunting began in childhood, when the school bus would stop at Kilnsey on the way to Littondale, Hubberholme or wherever, on one of those rare summer treats. The slope of the crag with its awesome overhang – used in training, we were always told, by Sir John Hunt's Everest heroes of 1953 – is so close anyone could hit it with a stone prised from the wall. No chance. Even the best thrower of a cricket ball among us could never get near.

In the teens there was a flirtation with climbing, nothing serious, more a walk with a bit of a stretch than anything like the Eiger. Kilnsey Crag boasts any number of routes of varying degrees of difficulty and, that overhang apart, does not look overly difficult. Until, that is, you stand at the bottom looking up. Forget it; let's go to the Tennant Arms and have a little lunch. No more climbing, vertigo did not have the chance to kick in.

Afew years later, when the delights of Kilnsey Show had been discovered – always at the end of August in the fields between the road and the infantWharfe – the mocking became yet more serious as the expert fell-racers battled their way to the top of the crag, then hurtled themselves fearless into the descent over scree and boulders to finish, proud and perhaps bloodied, back in the showfield. Even worse, the fresh-faced youngsters did the same thing, putting to shame those of us who had long since lost the desire – or the will – to run uphill. It is the same every time that road is used. There it is, standing there, silent but confident, knowing its strength, its place in the world. It's sad that such a magnificent sight should have been such an intractable opponent. **BB**

KING COAL

Who could ever have imagined that the day would come when Yorkshire had more doctors, lawyers or accountants than miners? Coal defined the language, lifestyle and landscape of vast swathes of Yorkshire, ran its mills, forges and factories, paid its bills, heated its homes and kept its lights burning. Coal was king, and when it was toppled from its throne it fell hard, taking thousands with it into a twilight of poverty. All the old iconic names of pits that were bywords for hard, sometimes dangerous, work and a breed of men who descended the shafts and came back up black-faced and exhausted became instead shorthand for deprivation, unemployment and desperation as communities came to terms with the loss of an industry that had sustained successive generations. Grimethorpe, Houghton Main, Brookhouse, Manvers, Hickleton, Markham Main, Prince of Wales, Wheldale, Sharlston and the rest – all the pits whose winding gear towered over their communities died one by one. And in their dying, all the coal towns, like Barnsley, Wakefield and Doncaster felt the pain. Prosperity went overnight, leaving behind it uncertainty and often the breakdown of social structures forged over a century or more. Pit villages had their own atmosphere, their own way of doing things, their own community spirit and values, all of them moulded by life down the mine. Often enough, they had their own mountain ranges too, as the houses looked across at the giant

Kilnsey Crag, near Grassington

KO (RICHARD DUNN)

It's said that when Muhammad Ali took off his gloves after defeating Richard Dunn (fifth round, fifth knockdown) written inside one was "Ali wins" and inside the other "round five". It didn't take a genius to forecast the outcome in the Olympiahalle in Munich on May 24, 1976. The 6ft 4in Bradford scaffolder, the British and Commonwealth heavyweight champion, was way out of his league in challenging for the world title. The silky skills of the greatest heavyweight boxer ever to step into a ring easily dealt with the Yorkshireman's clumsy southpaw rushes and Ali won on a technical knock-out. But Dunn had done good, so far as he was able, and a grateful city named its new sports centre after him on Odsal top. It was the site Richard Dunn had been working on before he went off to train for his Ali fight – which was to be the last of any significance in his career. Now 62 and somewhat arthritic, the grandfather of 11 is chairman of Scarborough Amateur Boxing Club in the town where he retired. **MH**

Frankie Dettori rides Sergeant Cecil to victory in the GNER Doncaster Cup at York on the first day of the St Leger Festival.

L

LASSIE

No-one much remembers Eric Knight – a one-time Yorkshire millworker – but they do still enjoy the most famous character he created. Nearly 70 years after Eric's piece of fiction, *Lassie Come Home* was published, the faithful rough collie was named top dog in a survey of 2,000 people. Eric Mowbray Knight was born in Menston in 1897, the son of a Leeds diamond merchant who abandoned his family and fled to South Africa. The family found themselves in much reduced circumstances and required a Plan B. Mother, who had worked for the Russian royal family, went off to St Petersburg to be governess to the children of Princess Xenia. Eric had to go and work for JB Farrar worsted spinners in Halifax – for a youngster with literary leanings it must have been something like the blacking factory for Charles Dickens. Eric escaped the mill at 15 when he was able to join his mother who had remarried and gone to live in Boston, Massachusetts. When the First World War came, Eric enlisted in the Canadian Light Infantry and after the war returned to the United States, working for several newspapers and later as a Hollywood scriptwriter. Yorkshire was never far away in his mind and he chose it as the setting for *Lassie*, published 1938. Eric wrote the screenplay and the film went into production in 1942. He never got to see it. In 1943, back in uniform as a US army officer, Eric was a passenger in an transport plane which crashed in the jungle of Dutch Guiana and killed the 34 people on board. **GH**

LAWRENCE, T.E.

To the men he worked with on Bridlington Harbour, and to the landlady of the privately-run Ozone Hotel, he was Aircraftman Shaw. They were all fond of the short, sandy-haired, soft-spoken man in his forties, all agreed that he had impeccable manners, and all were of a mind that he was an educated and engaging conversationalist, if one who preferred to listen to others while lingering over a half a bitter than offer his own opinions. Had he done so, they would have been taken aback at the scope of his vision of the world, especially the affairs of the Middle East, and his grasp of how power could be wielded for good or evil.

For Aircraftman Shaw was no ordinary serviceman.

The man whose job it was to maintain the RAF target boats used for bombing practice in Bridlington Bay had once commanded 200,000 men and changed the course of history, along the way becoming one of the most famous and féted men in Britain.

Thomas Edward Shaw was his real name, having changed it by deed poll in 1927. He had wanted to rid himself of the surname Lawrence, for the fame of being T E Lawrence, or in the public mind, Lawrence of Arabia, had become an unbearable burden. The story of how Lt Col Lawrence, Companion of the Bath, holder of the Distinguished Service Order, and the French Legion d'Honneur, the man who had fostered the Arab uprising against the Turks to aid British interests in 1916 and 1917, advised Winston Churchill on Arab independence and written two best-selling books, Seven Pillars of Wisdom and Revolt in the Desert, sought to escape the limelight in Bridlington is an extraordinary one. His fame appalled Lawrence, and he yearned for anonymity. He joined the RAF under the assumed name Ross in 1922, but was exposed and forced out. He managed to get in again in 1925, and starting in 1932 was periodically stationed at Bridlington for the next three years. He lived at the Ozone Hotel, and was endlessly enthusiastic about the motor boats he maintained and took out into the bay. If he talked about anything, it was about the boats. Some local people knew his real identity – he was one of the country's most-photographed men – but respected his wish for anonymity. Those who did attempt to draw him on his previous life were rebuffed with scrupulous politeness. Lawrence loved Bridlington for the low profile it afforded him, writing to a friend in November 1934: "A Christmas letter! To write it from the sea front of Bridlington at 10 at night with wind and rain outside and the long low-ride waves rolling up the sand feels somehow just right." Bridlington saw the last of him in March 1935 at the end of his RAF enlistment, when he set off from his lodgings by bicycle for the south of England. As he pedalled away, he shouted over his shoulder that he would be back for the summer. It was not to be. On May 13 1935, aged 46, Lawrence crashed his Brough Superior motorcycle on a quiet country lane near his cottage in Dorset, suffering serious injuries. Six days later, the extraordinary life of Aircraftman Shaw came to its close. **AV**

LEEDS LIBRARY

Only one thing counts on Commercial Street. Avid shoppers cruise up and down the thriving and anonymous thoroughfare which could be in any city, anywhere. Here, on one of Leeds's busiest streets but unnoticed and apart, is one of its great cultural assets, the Leeds Library. The *Yorkshire Post's* precursor, the *Leedes Intelligencer* once shared a home in this beautiful Georgian building which still offers an oasis of calm. Its front door swings shut on commerce and also, it seems, on the 21st century. Ahead is a flight of austere stone steps which lead up through a time warp into a setting created in 1808 and where the furnishings appear unchanged since 1908. It's quirky, cosy, cordial and possibly haunted. Anyway it's a gem. James Boswell in 1779 recorded his surprise at finding such an institution in Leeds and noted they treated him with great civility. This was one of the earliest proprietory subscriber libraries in the country – where the borrowers are the owners of the establishment – and the oldest surviving one. The librarian Geoffrey Forster is the man to ask about the causes of the Leeds dripping riots of 1865–1866 or why it once seemed a good idea to construct a celebratory arch over one of the city's main streets out of bread. The library opened on November 1, 1768 and moved to its present home in the summer of 1808, a century before public libraries. Dr Joseph Priestley, the discoverer of oxygen, was its first secretary and second president. Several of Charlotte Brontë's friends joined. No woman

Leeds Library.

got on to the committee, however, until the 1920s and it was only 10 years ago that they removed from the rules a reference to governesses being allowed in if their employers were members. Until 1990 family membership was set at 52p – the nearest convenient decimal equivalent to half a guinea. According to one published story, the ghost of a former librarian, Vincent Thomas Sternberg, haunted the place in 1884. In more recent times one of the cleaners has seen another ghost, this time a woman in grey. Even more interesting, there's a corner by a window to sit and make a cup of tea and where mince pies are laid on at Christmas.
MH

LIGHTHOUSES

They are the guardians of our coastline, the silent, untiring sentinels that have warned off generations of mariners from the rocks and cliffs that would claim their lives. In an age of global positioning systems, Yorkshire's lighthouses might be thought redundant. Not so. At Flamborough, Whitby and Scarborough, the lighthouses still flash out their messages into the night, and the crews of the vessels that ply the east coast are still glad to see them. The Yorkshire coast is dotted with lighthouses. Two remain at Spurn Point, though neither is in operation. Nor is Withernsea's most famous landmark, which stands in the centre of the town. Scarborough lighthouse has lent its name to where it stands, which is known as Lighthouse Pier, even though its proper name is St Vincent's Pier. Whitby Lighthouse stands just east of the town, and there are smaller lights on the east and west piers. But the best-loved of all Yorkshire's lighthouses must be Flamborough Head, which is the only one open to the public. Flamborough's lighthouse history goes back to 1669, when

Sir John Clayton built the 79ft chalk tower that still stands a little way back from the clifftop. Restoration work cast doubt on it ever having been used, and the Head had to wait until 1806 for the present lighthouse to be designed by Samuel Wyatt and built by John Matson. It was sorely needed – in the previous 36 years, 174 ships had been lost on the rocks of the headland, so the £8,000 it cost to build the 89ft tower and the attached keeper's house was money well spent. Flamborough was the first British lighthouse to show two white flashes and then a red from its oil-burning lamps. On foggy nights, it also fired rockets 600ft into the sky as further warning. These days, it shows four white flashes every 15 seconds that are visible 24 miles out to sea. Until 1996, keepers still lived there, but now Flamborough is fully automatic and controlled from the Trinity House depot in Harwich. Two hundred years on, it remains a vital waypoint for shipping, as well as one of the great landmarks of the Yorkshire coast.
AV

LIQUORICE

Better known as "lickrish" to small boys, a ha'penny liquorice root was one of the few treats available to kids in the post-war era at the sweet shop. The interesting stuff behind the counter was on ration. Once the end of the thin brown stick was sucked and softened, a reasonable amount of sweetness could be obtained if you worked at it. But hard chewing was subject to diminishing returns as the yellow fibrous inner root separated out. Liquorice pipes, strings, and other fancies were scoffed instead, once rationing finished. Even more desirable, but mostly aspirational, even in the times when we'd never had it so good, were Dunhill's Pontefract Cakes – moist, soft and and glossy

Flamborough Head lighthouse.

Malham Cove, a magnificent natural amphitheatre best seen from the air.

Rievaulx Abbey, the 13th century Cistercian ruin near Helmsley.

MEDITATION

Yorkshire's Abbeys

Some religious orders kept one foot in the cloister and one in the outside world, founding schools, caring for the sick in their hospitals and inventing things like watermills and windmills to make the land more productive. Others kept themselves to themselves. What they all shared, however, was a commitment to the interior life of the individual and the belief that this could be entered through prayer and meditation. These days the shells of what they created are often all that remain. But even a fleeting stop today at one of these sublime locations can leave a profound impression which in this unbelieving age can pass for spiritual. Two stars stand out. Fountains Abbey, a World Heritage site, is famous for its rose window and lovely geometric floor tiles. The Cistercians who built it named it after the springs in the area and it became one of the largest and richest houses in Britain. The biggest and most important monastery in England used to be Rievaulx, which is to be found in a dramatic setting near Helmsley. Older and more significant is Whitby, once home of St Hilda, and where in the 7th century the bishops came together to order that the Roman Catholic church have supremacy over the Celtic church. Bram Stoker chose the ruins as a suitable place for Count Dracula to make a landing. **MH**

MINING MUSEUM

School parties go there now, to learn about what life was like in the toughest, dirtiest, and maybe also the proudest, industry that ever grew up in Yorkshire. It's 22 years since the last coal came out of Caphouse Colliery, at Overton, near Wakefield, but it lives on as a memorial to the sheer courage and hard work of the heyday of Yorkshire's coalfield. It opened in 1988 as the Yorkshire Mining Museum, and was granted national status seven years later. And even among the county's distinguished roster of museums, it stands out. The cage takes visitors more than 400ft underground, where the workings are now galleries that give a unique insight into the long history of mining in Yorkshire. And Caphouse has one of the longest histories in Britain's coalfields. The shaft there first appears on maps dating from 1791, when it was in the ownership of the Milnes family. It passed through a series of owners until the coal industry was nationalised in 1947, and continued working until 1985, when the seam was exhausted. In 1983, the year before the miners' strike, the combined output of Caphouse and nearby Denby Grange was 383,000 tonnes a year, and every tonne dug returned a profit of £5.50. In its final years, the coal coming out of the New Hards Seam was brought to the surface at Woolley, seven miles to the south. Transforming Caphouse into the outstanding museum it has become was not easy. Minewater levels rose in 1997, and extensive work to pump the pit out and ensure its future had to be carried out by the Coal Authority. But since then, fund-raising by the museum totalling £2m and Lottery grants of more than £4.5m have done much to transform it into a magnet for visitors. It's an enormously evocative place, where the spirit of the generations of miners who worked at Caphouse hangs in the air. And nowhere is it more potent than at the bottom of that deep shaft where so many men embarked on another gruelling day at the coalface. **AV**

MYSTERY PLAYS

Where local girl Judi Dench started out (see above) when she was still a schoolgirl after the modern revival of the York Cycle of Mystery Plays in 1951. There's nothing mysterious about them. A "mystery" was a trade in the middle ages and in York the trades' organising and regulatory bodies, the guilds, were each responsible for putting on a play which illustrated something from the Christian tradition for the Corpus Christi festival. The authors were working men, and the plays gave them the chance to express their take on God and man using their own language, without it being mediated by the priestly caste through Latin. One manuscript survives, dating from around 1463–77, at the British Library. Over 40 wagons, each with its own play, used to rumble round the city every year until 1569 when the plays were banned because the Protestants had deleted the old Catholic festivals from the calendar. In the best of the York plays (other cycles also exist in Wakefield and Coventry) there's energy and humour and you hear the authentic voice of ordinary men speaking from over half a millennium ago. Others lack variation in language or characterisation and can be tedious. For many years, they were performed as a single programme in the Museum Gardens as part of the tri-annual York Festival with well-known actors in the main parts and local amateurs making up the rest – the York City Librarian once made a memorable Satan in the 1970s. The productions had the advantage of the wonderful backdrop of St Mary's Abbey, but after the first couple of hours on the temporary seating it could seem a bottom-numbing, and chilly, evening. Now the plays are usually done as they were meant to be, individually from wagons that process round the city and with the guilds back in charge. The Heritage Lottery Fund has been approached to see if they will fund a multicultural interpretation for 2012. **MH**

NAH THEN

It's taken me 30-odd years of living in Yorkshire to understand fully that a Yorkshireman (for it is more often a man) is not necessarily being challenging or confrontational when he says. "Nah then!" Sometimes he does deliver it to express an angry, frustrated feeling of "what's all this nonsense about?" But this is only one of many uses. Change the emphasis, and it's a warm, folksy and rather a neutral way to start a conversation. Used as a greeting, it's much better than the clipped "hello" or "hi" at implying an invitation to tell you news, or a readiness to hear some, and a willingness, if the time is right, to hang out for a bit. This is versatility of a high order and reveals the charm of a dialect typically determined to pack an optimum number of meanings into the fewest possible words. **SH**

NATIONAL PARKS

Britain's National Parks contain some of the most spectacular, most loved and carefully-protected scenery in Britain. Other counties feel flattered to host one of them. Yorkshire is unique in having two – three if you count the oldest, the Peak, which extends into South and West Yorkshire. And why not include it, since it was the energetic advocacy from the mid-1920s onwards, of a Sheffield woman, Ethel Gallimore, which did so much to prepare the public mind for the National Park concept? When the fighting ended in 1945, the government promptly put Ethel on a committee that six years later brought the Peak District National Park into being. Ten more were to follow in the coming decade, including the North York Moors in 1952 and the Yorkshire Dales in 1954. **GH**

NICHOLAS NICKLEBY

Even among fiction's bad boys – a crowded house of the nefarious and the abhorrent – Wackford Squeers is a conspicuous figure; so loathsome that he leaves a trail of slime behind him on the page. Charles Dickens sharply described Squeers as "much wrinkled and puckered up", and gave him a "sinister appearance". He brought unimaginable horror to the pupils of the Yorkshire boarding school, Dotheboys Hall, which Squeers sadistically ran in Dickens's *Nicholas Nickleby*. A character ignorant at one turn, (Squeers is illiterate) and inhuman at another, did not grow entirely out Dickens's imagination. Nor did Dotheboys Hall. And nor did the mistreatment and wanton neglect of the boys in it – "lank and bony" with "stooping bodies" and the "countenances of old men" – which Dickens captured so well

A school performance of Nicholas Nickleby

in his "Yorkshire novel". As a journalist, as well as a novelist, Dickens made *Nicholas Nickleby* into an example of reportage disguised as fiction. When Dickens wrote in Nickleby about the faces of the boys "darkened with the scowl of sullen, dogged suffering", he was drawing from raw experience. And the repulsive portrait of

Squeers was taken – fully fleshed and blunt boned – from a Londoner, who de-camped to Yorkshire, called William Shaw. Shaw ran the infamous Bowes Academy in North Yorkshire, where Dickens travelled to early in 1838 with his illustrator Hablot Browne (Phiz). From London's Snow Hill, it was a freezing, three-day, 255 mile journey on the

Penyghent in Ribblesdale in the Yorkshire Dales National Park.

Bakewell in the Peak District National Park, which extends into South Yorkshire.

rattling "Express" stagecoach. Already a celebrity, following *The Pickwick Papers*, Dickens had the ridiculous idea of adopting a pseudonym. Bogus letters of introduction were arranged. This pious fraud didn't work. Although Shaw met Dickens, he refused to speak to him or act as his guide around the Academy. Profitably tapping into anecdotal stories about the school, and reading the court documents from a successful prosecution of Shaw a few years earlier, Dickens pieced together a grim jigsaw of daily events: boys sleeping five to a bed on flea-infested mattresses, eating the scraps of maggot-riddled food, forced for days to go without clothes and, most vilely of all, confined for a month or more in the pitch-blackness of the Academy's wash-house for minor misdemeanours. Some went blind. Others died and were buried without ceremony, most in unmarked graves. *Nicholas Nickleby* brought volcanic change: Parliamentary debates, pupils withdrawn from schools, and those schools forced to close, including Shaw's miserable Academy. By 1864, a school commissioner was able to report: "I have wholly failed to discover one example of the typical Yorkshire School". **DH**

NIGHT SKY

and Fred Hoyle

The night sky is a site of special scientific interest and an area of outstanding natural beauty, but unlike the terrestrial sort, it's not so easy to protect. Urban light pollution obscures the view and some star-gazers have started a Campaign for Dark Skies which has supporters across Yorkshire. It wasn't too much of a problem for Fred Hoyle growing up in the village of Gilstead, in Brontë country, when there were no street lights at all. On Christmas Day 1925 Fred was given a

brass telescope and began experimenting. Alan Smailes, the headmaster of Bingley Grammar, spotted a star in the making and in December 1932 wrote to the Master of Emmanuel College, Cambridge: "The boy Hoyle has insight, energy and originality. He is young and his appearance is diffident and awkward ... I believe he will turn out to be a swan, no matter what sort of duckling or gosling he now appears." The headmaster was right. After the war, Fred became a radio celebrity, despite his gruff Yorkshire tones, and a best-selling science fiction author. His last years were overshadowed by an incident in Shipley Glen in November 1997, when he ended up face down in a stream, was not found for 12 hours and nearly died. He could remember nothing of it and might have been the victim of a mugger – £200 in his wallet was missing and a balaclava was discovered nearby. Afterwards, Fred complained: "I cannot multiply 57 by 32. I can get as far as the first multiplication, 57 X 3 = 171, but my ability to hold this intermediate result in memory is gone." When he died, aged 86, in 2001, the Astronomer Royal said Fred's insights into stars, nucleosynthesis, and the large-scale universe ranked among the greatest achievements of 20th-century astrophysics. **MH**

NINETEEN WICKETS

Jim Laker

The strip of black and white film, now more than half a century old, is just a few minutes long. It is grainy and a bit blurry too, as if you're looking at the action through grease-smeared lenses. But the Pathe News cameraman fortunate enough to be at Old Trafford over the last days of July, 1956 captured a piece of cricket history unlikely to be matched, let alone surpassed. This is the scene: Jim Laker takes 19 Australian wickets for 90 runs (9–37 in the first innings, 10–53 in the second) with a gentle, seven pace jog to the crease and a simple but fluid turn of his right arm. His off-breaks – delivered from around the wicket – bring bite, spin and varied bounce, and each success is greeted by the warm plummy tones of Pathe's Bob Danvers-Walker: "Bowled Laker!" Finally, there is Laker, sweater draped insouciantly over his left shoulder, shyly walking towards the camera. The last seven Australian wickets have fallen for eight runs in 22 balls. Improbable though it seems, the Yorkshireman who went on to play for Surrey – Laker was born in Frizinghall, Bradford in 1922 – began cricketing life as a fast bowler. Only the intervention of his coach BB Wilson, during an indoor net session, turned him into a spinner who shared in Surrey's seven successive County Championships in the 1950s. On the surface, Laker embodied the characteristics that those outside Yorkshire naturally associate with Yorkshiremen: blunt and tough to the point of occasional bloody-mindedness and unwilling to suffer the foolish or inept. But he was also a warm and considerate figure, too, always prepared to pass on advice and so knowledgeable and professional about the game that he soon became one of the BBC's most respected commentators. He died – far too young – aged 64 in 1986. **DH**

NORTH SEA

Holidaymakers love it, mariners respect it, and the people whose homes it claims curse it. The North Sea is the greatest force of nature visible in Yorkshire, alternately battering and caressing the coastline. It has been benevolent enough to feed the county, and merciless enough to swallow vast tracts of it. Its currents are among the most treacherous in the world, even on the days when it laps gently at sun-soaked beaches, and its tides can sweep into Flamborough or across Filey Brigg with an alarming rapidity that catches the unwary by surprise. Further south, it chops away at the soft clay cliffs with relentless force, taking eight feet of land a year and warning the people who live too close that their homes will, with the certainty of night following day, one day topple onto the sands below. It has periodically destroyed Spurn Point, only to rebuild it farther west, and claimed countless vessels that ply its endlessly busy shipping lanes. So the North Sea, with implacable power and inexhaustible energy, has sculpted the Yorkshire coastline as surely as it has shaped the lives of generations who have lived alongside it. The North Sea is far from being the prettiest in the world. Even on the brightest days, when the wave tops sparkle, it remains an obstinate grey, and when the spring and autumn tides sweep in with enough force to occasionally lift the boats out of Bridlington or Scarborough harbours, it can be downright ugly. It is relatively shallow, reaching a maximum depth of about 300ft off the Yorkshire coast, but that shallowness conceals some vicious undercurrents and makes it prone to producing some powerful wind-driven waves. These days, debates about the North Sea tend to focus on its erosion of the coastline and the state of its fish stocks. Over the next half-century, it is expected to claim more than 60 homes by eating into the cliffs, and if predictions about global warming and rising sea levels come true, massive defence systems will have to built to protect Scarborough, Filey, Runswick Bay and Whitby. The days when the North Sea, with its abundance of cod and herring, provided bountiful food for industrial Yorkshire are long gone. There was a time when the waters off the coast were so full of fish that boats from around Britain flocked there, lured by tales of cod that grew to eight feet long and weighed 200lb. Not any more. As fishing on an industrial scale has vacuumed up stocks, so has Yorkshire's fleet dwindled to a fraction of its former size. Yet the magical appeal of the North Sea endures for all those who witness it in its changing moods. To gaze on it from land or ship is to marvel at the power of Yorkshire's most restless and unpredictable neighbour. **AV**

NOWT

Nothing will come of nothing and nowt is less than that. It's not a shred, a ha'penny, jot or iota. The word sums up the economy and abruptness of Yorkshire speech. Those hard consonants sandwiching the flat vowel suggest the pleasure that can be derived from being dismissive. It also appeals to the instinctively parsimonious Yorkshire nature, since uttering it requires expending no more syllables than are absolutely necessary. Inevitably the word figures prominently in what detractors claim is the Yorkshire motto: "Hear all, see all, say nowt, tak' all, keep all, gie nowt, and if tha ever does ow't for nowt do it for thysen." **SH**

Spectator sport: watching the wild North Sea at Scarborough. Gary Longbottom

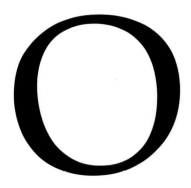

OINK

It's a popular notion that the East Riding has more pigs than people. It did, once. The pig industry had grown so large in the area because they had the land on which to put muck, straw on which to bed the pigs and the farm buildings manufacturers were handily based here. When the industry went through a bad patch many farmers didn't have enough money to renew, rebuild or refurbish so they packed up. Holderness alone once had 300,000 pigs. Today it's no more than 15–20 per cent of that. **MH**

OLD MOTHER SHIPTON

It was a dangerous time to be a witch between 1640 and 1662. So it's interesting that at the height of the feverish determination to persecute certain females, and have them done to death after a show trial, a pamphlet should appear in 1641 setting out the stall for just such a woman possessed of 'special powers'.Later a book appeared, claiming to tell her tale based on an old monastic manuscript. But *The Life and Death of Mother Shipton,* was a fake and fakery seems to have dogged the old lady's entire career, even though, in the beginning, it seems there was a real Mother Shipton in a cave in the Forest of Knaresborough in the later 15th century with a gift of prophecy. Her cave and a petrifying well are reckoned to be the oldest tourist attraction in the country and Mother Shipton's legend caught the attention of writers as diverse as Pepys and Dickens. **GH**

OLIVER'S MOUNT

Cromwell shelled Scarborough from its heights, Ann Brontë wrote wistfully of its beauty but it was Jack Claxton who brought fame to the hill between Seamer and Scarborough which is the only remaining natural road- racing circuit in Britain. Claxton had a dream. As secretary of the Scarborough and District Motor Club, founded in 1903 (the same year as the Auto Cycle Union), Claxton tried to persuade the town council to build a 10-mile racing circuit, on the lines of the Nurburgring in Germany to attract more visitors to the resort. The Thirties were lean times and when the cost of his project was put at £100,000 the council dropped it. Fast-forward to 1946 with Britain celebrating victory and the masses looking to relax after their tribulations. Claxton still had his dream, despite the shortage of fuel and racing motor-bikes. This time he persuaded the council to go ahead and in just six weeks a combination of grass tracks and farm roads had been transformed into a two-and-a-half

Motorcycle racer Bret Crossley from Castleford in action at Oliver's Mount

New Year's Day rainbow
viewed from Ilkley Moor.

mile black-topped circuit, complete with non-skid surface and five miles of telephone and loudspeaker wiring. The cost was under £1,000. Oliver's Mount was born and was soon established as the favourite venue of the great Geoff Duke and, later, Barry Sheene. In September 1953 39,980 people paid to watch Duke and John Surtees do battle; in 1970 Sheene and Yorkshire's Mick Grant drew 30,000 to Scarborough. All the great riders have ridden Oliver's Mount ; Bob McIntyre, Mike Hailwood, Phil Read, Giacomo Agostini, Joey Dunlop and Carl Fogarty among them ; and all were of one mind: Oliver's Mount was and is the best around for pure thrills. Thanks to Jack Claxton. BB

ON ILKLEY MOOR BAHT 'AT

Thomas Clark may have tapped out the first ideas for his tunes on a cobblers' last. He was a small businessman in the shoemaking trade in Canterbury and he would try out his compositions on the choir at at Wesleyan Methodist chapel in King Street where his family had long been members. Encouraged by their response, he felt confident enough to risk publishing his work and *A Sett of Psalm & Hymn Tunes with some Select Pieces and an Anthem* came out in 1805. Aimed at nonconformist congregations, Clark's published tunes were to be a big hit in the coming years. None has proved so enduring however as one in that first book called Cranbrook with words by Phillip Doddridge's beginning "Grace 'tis a charming sound". The story goes that in the 1860s, a church choir from Halifax went on a picnic to the Cow and Calf Rocks. The effect of the fresh country air on the young men and women prompted a certain loosening of Victorian corsets and an impulse to poke gentle fun at a favourite hymn. The result was a comic-lugubrious tale of a swain courting his love, Mary Jane, on Ilkley Moor through nine verses. The potentially fatal consequences of doing so without a hat (baht 'at) in such an exposed spot immediately struck a chord in the Yorkshire psyche which had nothing to do with religion. According to Charles H Dennis, a Huddersfield schools' inspector, the words of the song were picked up and sung in the area for the next two generations. Based on Dennis's recollections, *On Ilkley Moor Baht 'At* was published as sheet music for the first time in 1916 and then again, with the words which we generally use today, in 1927. Its appeal seems timeless and people throughout the world are familiar with what has become the National Anthem of Yorkshire, or at least the West Riding. For those unfortunate enough to have been born beyond those limits, but who wish to join in the singing, earn brownie points by hazarding the correct pronunciation: 'Ilkla Mooar'. **GH**

ONE HUNDRED HUNDREDTH

Geoff Boycott

"I saw it with amazing clarity and with something approaching elation. As soon as it left his hand, I knew I was going to hit it and I knew where I was going to hit it. Long before it pitched, I knew exactly what I was going to do, as though I was standing outside myself, watching myself play the shot. . .the ball hit the middle of the bat and went just past the far stumps on the on side . . . In the millisecond that followed I realised what it all meant . . . Somehow I was destined to get a century that day. It was my karma."

So said; and very eloquently too; Geoffrey Boycott when he described the "greatest moment" of his cricketing career. The date was August 11, 1977; the time was 5.47pm; the place was Headingley in front of what Boycott called "my people"; the match

was England v Australia; and the occasion was his one hundredth hundred. With Boycott on 96, Greg Chappell bowled him a medium paced half volley. Boycott lent into it, classically stroked the delivery for four to the long on boundary and became just the 18th batsman to complete a century of centuries ; and the only one to do so in a Test. Those who saw it, whether at Headingley or on TV, remember a jigsaw of images: Boycott with his arms aloft . . . Boycott almost submerged by the crowd rushing on to the parched, burnt outfield . . . Boycott losing his cap . . . the England team on the balcony . . . the unblemished cobalt sky . . . everything just perfect, and all played out to a symphony of noise too; an entire orchestra of Tyke voices; raucous, full-throated and loud enough to echo as far as Ilkley Moor. Only Boycott, the cricketing embodiment of Yorkshire grit and grind and perseverance, could have chosen his own home and an Ashes Test as a stage for such a sublimely personal achievement, which was more than 20 years in the dedicated making. "I was conscious I was sharing something important with the people of Yorkshire, " he said afterwards. "We just love him 'cos he's one of us, " explained a besotted spectator, illustrating the strength of the bond between Boycott and his public. Boycott later stood beside Herbert Sutcliffe and Sir Len Hutton, who had both made one hundred hundreds. The cameras clicked, the scene was frozen for posterity's sake and formalised; though it was hardly necessary; Boycott's place in Yorkshire's cricketing aristocracy.
DH

OPEN ALL HOURS

Stuttering Albert Arkwright was voted the nation's best-loved shopkeeper in 2007 in a poll of over 1,000 television fans. His Doncaster corner shop is now a tourist landmark even though it never really was an open-all-hours greengrocer's. The original location was Helen Ibbotson's Beautique Hair Salon at 15 Lister Avenue in Balby which had a make-over for the purposes of the show. It's creator, Roy Clarke, was once a Doncaster policemen and reckoned the job gave him more than enough first-hand experience of life to draw on to make a fulltime career as a writer. This show first made the screen in Seven Of One, a series of pilots featuring Ronnie Barker. When it got a run of its own, Barker was joined by David Jason as Granville, Arkwright's nephew the errand boy and together among the general stores and fruit and veg they lived a life of missed opportunities, their respective hopes of carnal and romantic satisfaction – in the direction of nurse Gladys Emmanuel from across the road and the milkwoman – doomed to perpetual frustration. Their end of town is now earmarked for 'reconstruction' and David Jason has signed a petition to prevent demolition of the shop, whose owner still plies her original trade of hairdressing.
MH

OXGODBY

JL Carr

"Oxgodby," calls the stationmaster as the train pulls level with the sodden platform. An gnarled old man in the corner of the carriage stares out of the window at the rain, falling in glassy sheets, and unnecessarily warns the stranger beside him: "Thoo's ga-ing ti git rare an' soaaked reet down ti hi skin, maister". This is Tom Birkin's terse welcome to Yorkshire in JL Carr's *A Month in the Country*; the best and most evocatively written post-war novel of the county. Birkin is a traumatised, stammering veteran of the

Great War now commissioned to restore the village church's medieval wall painting. He meets archaeologist Charles Moon, another twitching survivor of the trenches. Moon is scraping the grassy earth in search of a grave, and the explanation of why its occupant was buried outside the churchyard. The story essentially turns, however, on Birkin's attraction to the 19 year-old vicar's wife, who is as beautiful as a Botticelli painting. The story is told in first person; Birkin looks back regretfully over a period of "forty or fifty years" to the spring and summer of 1920. The book is elegiac, delicate, tender, achingly sad and powerful in imagery and symbolism, and its final lines stay with the reader and also convey the sense of time being "irrecoverably lost", which Carr intended. "We can ask and ask but we can't have again what once seemed ours forever," he writes. "We must snatch at happiness as it flies . . . " Carr set out to write an "easy-going story, a rural idyll along the lines of Thomas Hardy's *Under the Greenwood Tree*. He planted it in the North Riding and the Vale of Mowbray, where he was born in 1912 and his "folk" had lived for generations. But he modelled the church on one he knew in Norfolk, the vicarage from London and the fields from the countryside near his home in Northamptonshire. Joseph Lloyd Carr went to school in Carlton Miniott and at Castleford Secondary and he taught in South Milford, basing *How Steeple Sinderby Wanderers Won the FA Cup* on the village football team. He was a renaissance man; teacher and headmaster (until retiring in his mid-fifties to write novels), an artist, map maker, an antiquarian and publisher and polished amateur cricketer (he scored his last century at 57) and cricket enthusiast (*Carr's Dictionary of Extra-Ordinary Cricketers ; real and imagined*; is a miniature jewel). He was twice short-listed for the Booker Prize. Carr died of leukaemia in 1994. **DH**

OXYGEN

Oxygen was the discovery of the eminent Joseph Priestley and today in the West Yorkshire town where he was born they are keen to raise him to an ever higher pedestal. Most Friday nights his statue in Birstall town centre ends up with a can of beer in its hand so the plan is to elevate the great man out of harm's way and floodlight him. Priestley, 1733–1804, had a profound impact on the intellectual life of Leeds where he moved in 1767 to be the minister of the Unitarian Chapel at Mill Hill. He took up the study of chemistry and was one of the leading figures in the setting up of the Leeds Library which is still going strong. Moving to the West Midlands, he was part of the Lunar Society – clever chaps, such as Josiah Wedgwood, who met to discuss their scientific ideas on the night of the full moon so that they would have enough light to ride home afterwards. Priestley's radical thinking extended into politics and his sympathy for the ideas of the French Revolution incensed locals so much that a Birmingham mob broke into his house, wrecked his library and smashed up his laboratory. Priestley was valued more highly by the Americans after he moved there in 1794. As one of the writers of the US Constitution they regard him as one of the Founding Fathers and a man whose reputation emphatically deserves the oxygen of publicity. **MH**

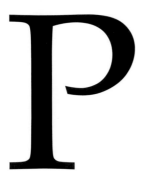

PALS BATTALIONS

They never had the chance to grow old.

The smiles and the friendships of the young men who flocked to the recruiting offices in Leeds, Bradford, Sheffield, Hull, Barnsley and Grimsby in the late summer of 1914 in response to an appeal to swell the ranks of Britain's army are forever frozen in the sepia-tinted photographs of the time. These were the 'Pals' battalions, volunteers who lived in the same streets and worked alongside each other in factories or offices, and who joined up together to form the backbone of a new army that would take the fight to the Germans on the Western Front. And these were the men who would perish in their thousands on the Somme in the summer of 1916. All the great industrial centres in Yorkshire raised Pals battalions. Barnsley sent two, as did Bradford. Leeds, Halifax, Grimsby and Sheffield sent one each. Hull raised four – Hull Commercials, Hull Tradesmen, Hull Sportsmen, and, with, wry humour, Hull T'Others. The men who joined spanned all classes.

Managers signed up along with men from the shopfloor. Miners from Charlesworth Colliery marched into Leeds to enlist, and formed the backbone of the Pioneers of the King's Own Yorkshire Light Infantry, becoming known as T'Owd Twelfth.

The famous were there too. Major William Booth, a rising star at Yorkshire County Cricket Club, joined up, as did left-handed batsman Roy Kilner. Leeds United and Bradford City star Evelyn Lintott, later to head the Professional Footballers' Association, became the first professional player to gain a commission in the Army. Training followed, and it was meticulous. It was above a year before the Leeds Pals were first deployed, to Egypt , and then in the spring of 1916, the Yorkshire Pals battalions found themselves bound for France. This was the build-up to Field Marshal Sir Douglas Haig's "big push" to break the German line at the River Somme, and one of his spearheads would be the 31st Division, which included the Pals from Leeds, Bradford, Sheffield, Barnsley, Durham and Accrington, who would attack on the first day of the battle, July 1 1916. Their objective was a sector near the village of Serre. The Accrington Pals went into battle first and were cut to pieces. The Leeds Pals followed, with 650 men going over the top at 7.30am. The horror of what followed lies beyond all imagining. The battalion lost 504 men and 24 officers. At roll call at the end of that terrible day, only 47 men answered. The 1st Bradford Pals lost 22 officers and 515 other ranks. The 2nd Bradford Pals lost 14 officers and 400 men. The Sheffield Pals lost half their strength. This was the single bloodiest day in

Members of The Great War Society representing The Pals Battalions of Leeds and Bradford march through the village of Bus Les Artois following the unveiling of a memorial to the Leeds Pals and Leeds Rifles.

British military history, and as night fell on the first day of the Somme, the army had sustained 57,470 dead or wounded. It took time for the news to filter back to Yorkshire. It was July 10 before Grimsby learned that half of the men it had sent to France would never return and, as the word spread of the carnage, a wave of grief and shock swept across the county. It was said that there was hardly a street in Leeds, Bradford or Sheffield that did not have at least one house where the curtains were drawn in mourning. There was more horror to come. The four Hull Pals battalions were held in reserve and escaped the slaughter of July 1. Their turn came on November 13, as the battle dragged on into its fifth month. With bitter irony, their objective was again the area around Serre, where the other Yorkshire Pals had suffered so grievously. The Hull Sportsmen and Hull T'Others went over the top first. By the end of the day, they had lost more than 800 men. The Pals who survived fought on for the rest of the war, but the distinctive nature of the Yorkshire battalions that had trained and marched together had been destroyed by the merciless slaughter. The Official History of the Somme saluted the "magnificent gallantry, discipline and determination" of the Pals on the first day of the battle, adding: "There was no wavering or attempting to come back. The men fell in their ranks, mostly before the first hundred yards of No Man's Land had been crossed." But it was one of the survivors, Private Arthur Pearson, of the Leeds Pals – whose life was saved by two tins of bully beef in his pack, which deflected a bullet – who summed up the horror and the futility of what happened most poignantly. "We were two years in the making and 10 minutes in the destroying."

AV

PEDAL POWER

Jane Tomlinson

Superlatives seem inadequate, but here goes. Jane Tomlinson was the most inspirational figure Yorkshire has produced in recent memory. Jane, from Rothwell, was diagnosed with breast cancer when she was 26 and she died, aged 43, in September 2007 after raising £1.5m for cancer charities.

She was a potent symbol of the human spirit at its most indomitable; her small round face and that slight frame conveyed a sense of extraordinary power because they were always to be seen at the conclusion of one of her extraordinary feats of physical endurance.

Each one was a defeat for adversity and never, even in death, did adversity win. The ending of her much-admired life marked a transition from a frail symbol of all that is best and brave to an indestructible one. Despite the fact that she knew her cancer was terminal, and that she suffered from chronic heart disease, Jane pushed herself to places that seemed far beyond the bounds of the possible. The biggest challenge she set herself came in the summer of 2006 when she cycled 4,200 miles across America. But she rarely finished her challenges without a triumphant, radiant smile; a smile which hid the deep heartache and very tough reality of her fight.

She was a plain-talking, strong-willed Yorkshirewoman who considered herself a wife, a mother, a grandmother, a daughter; a family woman. Publicly, Jane was often matter-of-fact about her illness. Cancer seemed simply to intensify her feisty and intensely proud nature, make her ever more determined to live what life she had and give everything her very best effort. Privately, of course, it was the source of great personal anguish.

Jane Tomlinson completes the Great North Run.

She was a spectator at the last sports event, a Leeds road race, held in her name and which she hoped would celebrate the city and Yorkshire and show people "just how fantastic they are". It did, and will continue to do so. For her legacy is an incredible ability to inspire others. **GH**

PEVSNER IN YORKSHIRE

Meticulous, fastidiously exhaustive and obsessive about architecture, no one knew more about the grandeur of Yorkshire's buildings than the German art historian Sir Nikolaus Pevsner, who was born in Leipzig in 1902 but escaped Nazism in 1934. He had an aesthetic eye, an appreciation for craftsmanship and never lost his sense of awe at a wellshaped finial or a spire spearing the sky. His series *The Buildings of England* is a monument of ink and paper. Pevsner set out, starting after the Second World War, to create an easily read and portable guide. He wrote 47 volumes on England (some with contributors) and the early publicity blurbs described them without fuss or hype as "full particulars of the architectural features of all ecclesiastical, public and domestic buildings of interest in each town and county . . . "

At first, he travelled the highways and byways in a 1933 Wolseley Hornet borrowed from his publishers Penguin and driven by his wife. By the late, "you've never had it so good" 1950s, he caught up with Yorkshire, and split the county into three: *The West Riding* (1959) *The North Riding* (1966), *York and East Riding* (1972). The books total more than 1,500 pages, and provide irresistible detail on everything you ever want to know about hipped roofs, mullions and flying buttresses. Pevsner particularly relished the North Riding, calling it "a wonderful county ... the enjoyment enhanced by the people, so genuine, so hospitable. The South has nothing to equal them . . . "

Pevsner died in 1983 after a lifetime of dedicating his guides to "those publicans and hoteliers of England who provide me with a table in my bedroom to scribble on". **DH**

PIECE HALL

We treasure our historic buildings in a way that previous generations were sometimes less enthused and the results can be seen across the county, nowhere better perhaps than in the marvellous Piece Hall in the centre of Halifax.

Opened for business on January 1 1779, this unique building – others of its like in Leeds, Huddersfield, Bradford and Wakefield having long since been demolished – was a centre at which weavers, who worked in their cottages in the surrounding villages and hamlets, could sell their cloth "pieces" to merchants. Market day was Saturday and the hours of business were strictly controlled, anyone buying or selling outside the permitted hours incurred a fine. The rapid growth of the woollen industry in the Halifax area – which overtook Ripon as the largest centre of production in Yorkshire, five times larger than Leeds and eight times bigger than Bradford – ensured that trade was brisk. Piece Hall was built at a cost of £12,000, the money being raised through subscriptions, each costing £28, which provided access to a small room with a door and window. For those unable to raise the funds to subscribe, there was the option of selling their cloth in the courtyard. The demand for a Piece Hall began to wane in the early years of the 19th century with the coming of the mills, which allowed the merchants to buy all they needed from one or two sources and in 1815 the rules of business were changed to allow cotton as

Halifax Piece Hall.

well as wool to be traded. The decline continued and in 1868 Piece Hall was handed over to the local authority, who reopened it in 1871 as a wholesale fish, fruit and vegetable market. Its historic importance was, thankfully, recognised and in 1928 Piece Hall was declared an ancient monument but it was not until 1972 that it was accorded Grade I listed building status, removing any threat of demolition. Renovation work began and the Piece Hall was reopened for business on Saturday July 3, 1976 and is still a working market with stalls offering all manner of goods. **BB**

PLATH THE POET

The grave is plain and inconspicuous, and difficult to find. The inscription on the granite headstone – in neatly chiselled capitals – reads:

IN MEMORY
SYLVIA PLATH HUGHES
1932 – 1963
EVEN AMIDST FIERCE FLAMES
THE GOLDEN LOTUS CAN BE
PLANTED

To the Church of St Thomas in the hilltop village of Heptonstall, just outside Hebden Bridge, poetry lovers make a pilgrimage to stand beside the grave and frequently to argue over it. All because the life of Sylvia Plath – born in Massachusetts, found dead in London and buried in Yorkshire – became the stuff of raw tragedy, and of the sort Shakespeare once turned into stage drama. A colossal talent who commits suicide after her better known poet husband, Ted Hughes, leaves her for another woman. A posthumous, shining fame from the publication of confessional poetry, and intimate journals and letters. And a feuding

saga around the unquiet grave: the lead spelling out Hughes's name repeatedly levered off the headstone by his feminist detractors, and the headstone removed for more than a year in the late 1980s for restoration. Hughes was vilified for neglecting her memory, for breaking up the marriage, for tampering with and/or suppressing her work, for burying her in Yorkshire rather than Cornwall and for, well, just being Hughes. Even after becoming Poet Laureate, he had to argue against the grave being signposted. He spoke of his "horror of what will happen when Sylvia Plath's grave becomes one more trampled Disneyland" and "hawked in brochures". The fascination for Plath and her work continues nonetheless. The fact is that, during the bitingly hard winter of 1963, shortly before sealing herself into the kitchen of her London flat and switching on the gas, she wrote some of the best poetry since the end of the War. Hughes buried his wife in Heptonstall, which he described in the poem Wodwo as the "black village of gravestones," because it was near his family home. Plath had relished the Yorkshire countryside. Writing to her mother, she called it an "incredible, wild green landscape of bare hills, crisscrossed by innumerable black stone walls like a spider's web ..." On the day of her funeral, snow lay across that greenery and those walls. Only months before his own death in 1998, Hughes published *Birthday Letters*: 88 poems of which all but two detailed, and strive to explain, his relationship with Plath. His ashes were scattered on Dartmoor and a long slab of granite, his name engraved on it, was laid on its northern edge near the source of the River Taw. **DH**

The quotation on Plath's headstone was chosen by Hughes, who always said it came from the Bhagavadgita. It is actually found in Wu Ch'Eng-En's Monkey, written in the middle of the 16th century.

PUDSEY'S SIR LEN

If Yorkshire is the capital of cricket, (and who would dare argue otherwise?), then Pudsey is the capital of cricket in Yorkshire. It has, as the magazine *Wisden Cricketer* once made clear, produced a "better cricketing education" than any public school. The evidence is overwhelming.A bat, a ball and a set of stumps ought to be on the town crest. It has produced two Ashes winning captains, Sir Len Hutton and Ray Illingworth, as well as prolific runmaker Herbert Sutcliffe and bowler Matthew Hoggard. Scant wonder that, shortly after the War, the music hall joke was "Where's Leeds?", and the answer came back: "Near Pudsey".

The most stellar of Pudsey's cricketing sons is, very obviously, Sir Len. Born 1916 in the Moravian village at Fulneck, he was met at his first Yorkshire net session by the legendary George Hirst, who said simply: "You're the boy from Pudsey . . . "

He learnt his trade at Pudsey St Lawrence CC's homely Tofts Road ground. The club's gates are dedicated to him, and a corner of the pavilion – the view from it dominated by the tower of St Lawrence Church – contains a mini-shrine. There is a print of him in his pomp, assorted framed photographs (meeting the Queen, being congratulated by Don Bradman) and a bail from the Australian Test at the Oval in 1938, during which he stroked what was then a history-making 364. It remains the highest score in any Ashes match. Sir Len revealed a steely and single-minded devotion to the game. He joined Pudsey in 1931, made his Yorkshire debut three years later, his Test debut in 1937 and became the first professional captain of England in 1952. He regained and then retained the Ashes in the early and mid-1950s, retiring in 1955 with 129 centuries. The knighthood soon followed. If Hitler hadn't been rude enough to re-arrange the summer fixture list – and if Sir Len hadn't damaged his left arm so badly during the War that it became two inches shorter than his right – the hard statistics of his career would have soared off the chart. He was 23 when War broke out, and 30 when first-class cricket eventually resumed. As the *Yorkshire Post's* cricket correspondent JM Kilburn wrote, Sir Len nevertheless carried "factual achievement beyond the acceptable limits of romance". He died, aged 74, in 1990. **DH**

PUPPETS

Sooty and Sweep

It was on a rainy summer's day on Blackpool's North Pier in 1948 that a showbusiness legend was born.Ayoung electrical engineer called Harry Corbett, from Guiseley, near Leeds, spotted a yellow glove-puppet bear in the window of a novelty shop and bought it for 7s 6d. He thought it would make his young son, Matthew, laugh and might also find a place in the amateur magic act that boosted Corbett's meagre income. At the suggestion of his wife, Marjorie, he blacked up the bear's ears with soot to make him look more distinctive. The name Sooty followed naturally. Sooty made his debut at a children's party in Pudsey Masonic Hall, where he was the star of the show.

Corbett then landed a slot on a BBC showcase for amateur talent and took Sooty with him. He was such a success that the BBC offered him a series of six programmes at 12 guineas a show. That was in 1952, and within a couple of years Sooty was the hottest attraction on children's television. It was an unlikely success. Sooty never spoke, preferring to whisper in Corbett's ear, periodically squirted him in the face with a water pistol and played the xylophone. But the kids went mad over him, and Corbett

was shrewd enough to spot he was onto a winner. In 1955, Sooty made the front pages for scoring a direct hit on the Duke of Edinburgh with his water pistol at London's Olympia and his fame shot up once again. The cast of characters was gradually expanded. Sweep, the squeaky-voiced sidekick appeared in 1957, and in 1964, Soo the panda made her debut and immediately caused a row, with the BBC complaining that she added an unsavoury whiff of sex to Sooty's wholesome image. It even rewrote Corbett's contract to ensure that there was never any contact between the two. Corbett ploughed on, adding such other sterling supporting players as Ramsbottom the snake – who had a broad Lancashire accent – Butch the bulldog, and PC Nab, whose regular humiliation prompted a delegate to the Police Federation to complain that Sooty was undermining respect for the law. The relationship between Corbett and Sooty was close to the point of obsessive. Corbett always ensured Sooty laid face up in the box in which he travelled and even drilled air holes in the lid so he could breathe. He once set off with his family on holiday, and five

miles from Guiseley cried "I can't go without him," then turned round and went back to collect Sooty. Corbett parted company with the BBC in 1968 after a row which was as comical as anything Sooty did.

The Corporation suggested that a younger presenter was needed, and when the avuncular, balding Corbett refused, they suggested that he wore a toupee, hinting that otherwise Sooty might go the way of Pinky and Perky, who had just been axed. ITV snapped Sooty up, and it was plain sailing until Corbett suffered a heart attack in 1976 and handed over Sooty to Matthew. That same year, he received the OBE, and at the investiture, the Queen reportedly said to him: "I must say I like the bit where Sooty hits you over the head with a hammer." An embarrassed Corbett explained that he had dropped that routine after a watching toddler had hit his father over the head with a real hammer. Corbett said his final "Bye, bye everyone. Bye, bye" in 1989 at the age of 71. But Sooty endures. He's still touring, still packing out theatres, and still enchanting children. The last silent star has become one of the great showbiz survivors. **AV**

Len Hutton (left) with Frank Lowson.

QUAKERS

Quakers, The Society of Friends preach pacifism, temperance and simplicity and it was in Yorkshire that their national yearly meetings began. Ironically, these peaceable men who came here to spread the word often got into public punchups. William Dewsbury, who proclaimed in Settle, for example, was set-upon by the crowd. Quakers are diligent, careful, mild people and often do well in life. The chocolate makers Fry (Bristol), Cadbury (Bourneville) and Rowntree (York) helped endow Quaker schools like Ackworth, near Pontefract, and The Mount and Bootham in York. In that city Quakers have long fed the mind and tempted the sweet tooth. The first Joseph Rowntree bought his grocers' business from a Tuke, a Quaker family who set up the first enlightened mental hospitals, Bootham Park and the Retreat. The ground-breaking research of Joseph's grandson, Seebohm Rowntree, revealed a degree of poverty in the city so severe and widespread it made national headlines at the turn of the 20th century. A Liberal, Seebohm played a key part in helping win the First World War. His old pal, the Prime Minster Lloyd George, put Seebohm in charge of the armaments factories and the enlightened working methods pioneered at the Cocoa Works in York were introduced elsewhere in place of strife. The mark that Seebohm left post-war was more permanent – he was one of the main architects of the Welfare State. Unlike most captains of industry, the self-effacing Seebohm declined to boast about his achievements. When approached about receiving honours he declined on the grounds that he could not accept anything that put a distance between himself and his fellow men. **FM**

QUARTERDECK

Mutiny on the Bounty and the career of Charles Laughton

"Mister Christian!" That unmistakable voice, heavy with menace was accompanied by a baleful stare from those poached-egg eyes. He was, in 1935, the man that cinema audiences loved to hate. Charles Laughton, son of Scarborough, pacing about the quarterdeck of *HMS Bounty* in the role of Captain Bligh, being beastly to an unusually un-moustachioed Clark Gable as Fletcher Christian. *Mutiny on the Bounty* was Laughton's first great gift to Tony Hancock and several generations of mimics. There was to be another boon to the impressionists four years later, in 1939. "The bells, the bells," Laughton cried as Quasimodo in *The*

Joseph Rowntree

Charles Laughton as
Quasimodo in The Hunchback
of Notre Dame

Hunchback of Notre Dame, sealing his place as one of the finest screen actors. His was a long, sometimes wayward, and often triumphant career. That jowly face – he once compared it to an elephant's behind – could radiate menace or warmth and in an era where filmgoers were accustomed to clear-cut heroes or villains, Laughton's characters exuded ambiguity and emotional depth.

Laughton knew how good he was, and knew also how to suggest darker motives in his characters, remarking: "They can't censor the gleam in my eye."

There is a blue plaque commemorating him on the wall of the Victoria Hotel in Scarborough, where he was born on July 1, 1899. Amateur dramatics consumed him, and the increasing prosperity of the Laughtons in Scarborough's hotel trade allowed him to attend RADA in 1925. A year later, he was taking leading roles in the West End and his Hollywood debut was in 1932 in *The Old Dark House*. There were wobbles, poor films and mutterings of over-acting along the way, but as Laughton approached 60, the world rediscovered its admiration for him and he was nominated for an Oscar in 1957 for *Witness for the Prosecution*. He took American citizenship but just watch him in his penultimate film, *Spartacus* and listen to those vowels. Aboy could be taken out of Scarborough, but Scarborough could never be taken out of the boy. **AV**

QUEEN'S COUSIN

The Earl of Harewood, of the eponymous grand house between Leeds and Harrogate, is a first cousin to the Queen. His father, Viscount Henry Lascelles, married Princess Mary, daughter of George V. Mary's brother became George VI. Henry and Mary were married in 1922 and their son and heir, George, was born a year later. Henry became

an Earl in 1929 and in 1930 the couple moved into Harewood House, Henry dying in 1947 and his countess in 1965. George Lascelles, seventh Earl of Harewood, vigorously embraced the arts (artistic director of both the Royal Opera House and Edinburgh Festival, a founder of Opera North). Less happily these days, he is the president of Leeds United football club. He has four sons and now lives with his second wife at Harewood which dates from 1759 and is a treasure trove of pictorial art furnished with outstanding Chippendale furniture. Day-to-day estate decisions are in the hands of his heir, David, a film-maker. Among his producing credits are the fourth and fifth series of *Inspector Morse* – a total of nine Morse episodes in all – including the very last one when the inspector dies. The family presents a three-week Caribbean Carnival in September, based on Handel's *Messiah*, celebrating the abolition of slavery. It was money from the West Indian sugar plantations that enhanced the family fortune. **FM**

QUEEQUEG

"Call me Ishmael," says the narrator at the opening of *Moby Dick* as he arrives at the seafarers' Spouter Inn in New Bedford to discover his room-mate is Queequeg, a fearsome South Sea Islander covered with tattoos who uses his razor-sharp harpoon to shave himself. Oddly enough, the pair's fictional destinies are bound up with a real 58-foot sperm whale which got stranded on the beach at Tunstall, north of Hull in 1825. The law said it belonged to the Lord Paramount of the Seigniory of Holderness, Sir Clifford Constable, who had the dead whale removed to Burton Constable Hall where its skeleton became a talking point in the grounds. Thomas Beale, a surgeon,

Guest appearance: After luncheon at Harewood House on October 20, 1958, the Queen and the Duke of Edinburgh pose with some of the members of the house party, Front row, from left: The Earl of Harewood, the Duke of Edinburgh, The Queen, the Princess Royal, the Hon Gerald Lascelles. Back row: The Countess of Harewood, Prince and Princess Louis of Hesse and the Rhine and the Hon Mrs Gerald Lascelles.

Laurence Sterne.

naturalist and whaler, came to view it and wrote a definitive book, *The Natural History of the Sperm Whale*, in 1839. Ten years later, Herman Melville, a sailor and would-be writer, picked up a copy on the other side of the Atlantic and plundered much of the scientific info to give ballast to his metaphysical musings in *Moby Dick*. Noone took too much notice until early 20th century writers acclaimed Melville as the first great white hope of the American novel. Gregory Peck, a memorable Captain Ahab in the 1956 film, fixed the story more firmly in the public imagination, becoming the prototype for Jaws. The monster whale finally does for the obsessive Ahab, his ship the *Pequod* and poor old Queequeg, too. The real one, unseen for a century, has just been cleaned up and put back on public show in Burton Constable's Great Hall. **MH**

QUIRKY

Laurence Sterne and Tristram Shandy

It's funny how enduring country memories can be. "He fell through the ice in the village and no-one pulled him out." "Abit of a weasel really." The man these anonymous quotes refer to died 200 years ago. Laurence Sterne was the vicar of Coxwold who wrote *The Life and Opinions of Tristram Shandy, Gentleman*. Clever, bawdy and constructed so as to confuse the literary expectations of dull readers, it was published between 1759 and 1767 in nine volumes, the last appearing just before Sterne died. He was 46 when he began the tale – supposedly the autobiography of Tristram Shandy starting on the night his parents go to bed and conceive him. But the outside world keeps breaking in on his narrative and he does not get himself born until the fourth book. It concludes with him giving up and admitting to the reader it has all been a cock and bull story.

Sterne's friends gave the name Shandy Hall to his house – shandy then being a Yorkshire term for "barmy". Today, it is one of the quirkier gems of Yorkshire thanks to the magnificent barminess of the Monkmans, Kenneth and Julia, who made a pilgrimage to Coxwold in the 1960s and discovered the hall had been a farmhouse for 200 years. They acquired it and painstakingly recreated the Shandy Hall Laurence Sterne had known.

The result is part family home, part literary shrine and is so thoughtfully done it seems as if Sterne is still present but has just popped out to do a bit of gardening. Aquill

A quoits player from 1957, one of the images in an exhibition called "Work Hard Play Hard" at the National Mining Museum near Wakefield.

pen, casually laid aside next to the inkwell in his study, is the finishing touch. It has something for everyone, whether their interest is history, horticulture or the Age of Enlightenment. Comedian Steve Coogan helped popularise Sterne with his recent film *A Cock and Bull Story*. Rather too late though to win over the opinions of those locals who had known the man himself. **MH**

QUOITS

That clanking sound you hear is the noise of a five pound piece of iron with a hole in the middle hitting a pin. If it goes over the pin it's a ringer.

This is quoits – not the girlie sort, flinging a bit of rubber about the deck of a cruise ship – but a proper man's game dating from the time when we still had heavy industry. You needed good muscles to get a grip on the traditional quoit the size of a dinner plate made from malleable iron with a weight limit of five-and-a-quarter pounds, and hurl it the required distance of nine yards. The pitch, pin to pin, is 11 yards but the rules allow the thrower to take two strides.

The winner is the first to go 21-up and although a ringer scores two points, that's not the main aim because it's counted out if another ringer is planted on top. What you need to do is get your quoit in front of the pin in a position where an opponent can't score. Iron mining and smelting used to be big on the North York Moors which may explain why the game has persisted so long around here. The Danby and District Quoits League and the North York Moors League have mostly the same players and compete under North of England rules, with slight local variations. The Birch Hall Inn Club at Beck Hole – where there were pitches in their present position in 1882 – is one of the main outside venues for league matches from May to August.

There's also a knock-out cup whose final is in August with 10 teams competing. In winter, they keep their hand in with indoor games on Mondays at the Whitby Rifle Club. Bill Cockerill, joint secretary and treasurer of Beck Hole, has been involved since the early 1950s. Bill says the game has died a little bit because no young players have come on in the past 10 years. **MH**

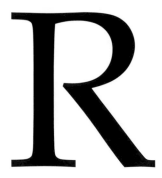

RIDINGS

The Ridings, derived from a Norse word meaning third, had stood the test of time. The 2,775 square miles of the West Riding swept down from Sedbergh to Sheffield, enclosing the southern Yorkshire Dales plus the industrial heartland around Leeds and Huddersfield to reach the Nottinghamshire border. The more lightly populated North Riding (2,128 sq m) reached up to Redcar and enclosed the northern dales and North York Moors. The East Riding took the 1,172 sq m that were left, from just below Scarborough to Goole. The Ridings could not stand the test of 'rationalisation' imposed in 1974 by local government reorganisation. For rational read perverse. Places like Sedbergh and Middlesbrough, with a quarter of the North Riding populace, ended up in other counties with new names, Cumbria and Cleveland. Much of the East Riding became North Humberside (which has since been 'reorganised' again). Some of it, bizarrely, became North Yorkshire, even reaching areas below Selby which in terms of culture and outlook are part of the South Yorkshire coalfield. This new North Yorkshire was huge, also gathering the upper part of the old West Riding. The old West Riding areas of Barnsley, Doncaster, Sheffield and Rotherham went into the newly-minted South Yorkshire.

It antagonised many and out of that feeling grew the Yorkshire Ridings Society which levered an agreement that the new regions were not a necessity in postal addresses – just Yorkshire and the post code were sufficient. The society's seven-point Yorkshire Code advises that the Ridings were not legally abolished. It is doubtful today whether the demise of the name Ridings or the jiggling with boundaries has any import for most people under 40 years of age. It could have been worse, it was certaintly rather pointless. If local government needed reordering it could have been achieved without ditching the titles of those ancient Thirds. **FM**

RINGERS

and York Minster

It's 99 winding steps up the south west tower of York Minster to the bell-ringing chamber. Ten ringers approach their appointed rope and stand gravely for a moment and then, without any obvious signal, begin. It seems quite off-the-cuff, bearing in mind that any blunders are going to be picked up (by anyone who knows anything about bell ringing) across broad swathes of the Vale of York. The 12 Minster bells have 479,001,600 different changes, and the sequences – called "methods" have to be memorised. To ring a

Ringing Master Tim Bradley at York Minster.

Janet Oldroyd checks some of her rhubarb at her farm at Carlton. Simon Hulme

full peal at the Minster takes four to four-and-a-half hours and involves 5,088 changes rung in strict order without repeating any. The tenor bell which acts like a drumbeat in the rhythm, weighs three tons and it's the diameter of a bell and the thickness of the metal which determines its harmonics. As they prepare to ring in the New Year, crowds now gather at the front of the Minster, a fairly recent innovation. Making some sort of music here pre-dates the ringers. The first Minster song school may have been as early as AD 627, some 600 years before the building we see today was completed. Some of the songmen who lived at the adjacent Precentor's Court were among the first on the scene in the early hours 9 July 1984 when a lightning struck, destroying the roof of the South Transept and shattering the famous rose window. That part was all restored good as new and now pots of money, they hope £30m, will be spent in coming years on the rest. The bill for repairing the stained glass in the East Window – which cost £56 in 1405 – will be £6m. How's that for price inflation? The exterior has stayed good-looking because of milk. For cosmetic effect, Victorian stonemasons applied to the Minster's limestone a mixture of sour milk, ochre and lime which turned out to be a preservative. **MH**

RHUBARB

It's not a fruit but a vegetable and first came to notice in 2700BC on the Russia/China border. Parts of the rhubarb plant have been used to treat everything from stomachache to venereal disease and the Victorians valued it as a purgative. Yorkshire has traditionally been a centre for it and today the National Rhubarb Collection is held at RHS Harlow Carr near Harrogate. Once 200 growers thrived in the "golden triangle" between Leeds, Bradford and Wakefield producing 5,000 tons a day. Forced rhubarb is cultivated outdoors for two years before being moved into special sheds where it's harvested by candlelight. Regular rhubarb trains used to depart Wakefield for London full of the stuff but it was left on the shelf when more exotic imported fruits arrived on the scene. It has since staged a come-back as a "superfood" – low in carbohydrate, high in vitamins, and said to help slimming. Nigella Lawson swoons over its sensuality and comforting qualities and traditional rhubarb crumble features on the menus of posh restaurants. The twelve West Yorkshire growers who remain are now attempting to get Protected Designation of Origin (PDO) status from the EU. **GH**

ROBIN HOOD

They gave it the name Robin Hood, even though it's nowhere near Nottingham. And everyone knows that's where Robin Hood belongs because his bronze statue stands in the shadow of Nottingham Castle where his foe, the evil sheriff, used to hang out. So is the old RAF Finningley near Doncaster headed in the right direction? The people who run it now think so because like John Lennon airport (formerly Liverpool-Speke), Robin Hood rings a bell with people scanning distant departure boards where knowledge of England is sketchy. On the other hand, the airport's main operator, Thomsonfly, prefers to call it Doncaster on its poster adverts which really is what it is. But what's in a name? The main thing is that the new enterprise promises to lift up-and-away the economy of this area left down and almost out when the coal industry collapsed. The huge runway, built to accommodate RAF bombers, is unique in the north. Success is not just flying locals out, but also about puffing-up the area for people who might come in. New arrivals who want to pick up on the Robin Hood myth might will have a bit of a journey, although it doesn't have to be to Nottingham. The original Hoodie first lurked in Sherwood Forest when it stretched up into Yorkshire, probably in the Barnsdale area and convenient for the A1. A ballad called *A Lytell Geste of Robyn Hode* written in the first half of the 15th century, mentions Doncaster, Kirkleees Priory and Wentbridge. The balladeers may have exploited the Nottingham connection some time later to increase their chart sales. **MH**

ROCK IN YORKSHIRE

The definitive Yorkshire rock gig may have been The Who Live in Leeds. Jimi Hendrix live in Heslington and not-so-live in Ilkley must have provided two of the oddest. The unknown Jimmy Hendrix arrived in London in late September 1966 from New York. Within a week the newly-named Jimi was a star and Eric Clapton, sitting in the audience for the first show, excused himself to go home and practise. The York University site at Heslington consisted of two prefab-built colleges, Langwith and Derwent, and the announcement that Hendrix was coming went up on their notice boards along with the sports and social clubs' meetings in February 1967. Langwith dining room was the venue. Hendrix, arriving late on a Friday night, played on a makeshift stage. He was within touching distance of anyone who wished to try, although in those days people preferred to dance in the presence of a rock god, rather than stand awestruck. The following month Hendrix was back in Yorkshire at the ballroom of the Troutbeck Hotel, Ilkley. It was Sunday night, the place was packed. As Hendrix prepared to play a chord, a member of the constabulary

elbowed his way to the front of the stage and announced the numbers present constituted a fire-risk. Unless some people volunteered to leave the building, he would pull the plug. They didn't, so he did. The disgruntled crowd surged out, many of them bearing bits of the ballroom furnishings above their heads. **MH**

ROSE (WHITE)

White is the symbol of purity, a quality which is mostly aspirational for the majority of the people born within the White Rose county today. It's said that Edmund of Langley, the first Duke of York, made a white rose his badge – it also had associations with the Virgin Mary, Mystical Rose of Heaven – although the Duke did not actually have much to do with Yorkshire. The white heraldic rose handily identified the forces of the house of York when they went to war with people on the other side of the Pennines whose rose emblem is still believed to be red. The combatants never called it the Wars of the Roses, a term dreamed up hundreds of years later by Sir Walter Scott in Ivanhoe. The slaughter reached its peak at Towton near Tadcaster on a snowy Palm Sunday, on March 29th, 1461. This was the bloodiest encounter ever on English soil, and in terms of the numbers killed as a proportion of the population, the battle was akin to the mass blood-letting in World War I. Over half of the 28,000 men – including the flower of the English nobility – died in a frenzy of hacking and mutilation. Modern research on some of the bodies revealed the soldiers were big and fit and the multiple injuries they received were far greater than were necessary to kill them. Noses and ears were routinely severed. The Yorkists were victorious but it wasn't to last. The conflict resumed in 1470 and it's still going strong with the cricket arena hosting the main encounter. In 2007, on home turf, the white rose was humbled as never before, although it was an Australian, laying about the Yorkies with a flashing blade, who gave most help to the other side in achieving its triumph. **MH**

RUDSTON MONOLITH

There is a tale of Satanic fury that goes back a millennium in the rolling hills of the Yorkshire Wolds._The Devil, it is said, was so maddened by the sight of a church built on the hill at Rudston that he hurled a spear at it. Evidently, either Satan's aim was off or a righteous hand intervened, and he missed by 12ft, his stone spear embedding itself in the ground as both a warning to the ungodly and a silent testament to the power of good. And there Satan's spear still stands – the Rudston Monolith, 25ft and 9ins of silent witness to an age where Christianity and paganism jostled for the upper hand. It is Britain's tallest standing stone, dwarfing Stonehenge, and its story is hardly less remarkable than the fable of the Devil's temper tantrum. It dates from around 1600BC, and is a solid piece of gritstone, the nearest outcrop of which is at Cayton Bay, about 10 miles across hilly country. Excavations by Sir William Strickland in the 1700s suggested that there is as much of the monolith below ground as above it, raising the astonishing prospect that the ancients quarried and dragged a 50ft monument across country. Archaeologists have also theorised that glacial movements much earlier may have deposited the stone on the Wolds. Whichever – or neither – is correct, the act of getting it into the arrow-straight position it has held for more than 3,000 years atop a hill is a feat to wonder at. It was a landmark by the early 1100s, when All Saints Church was built next to it, in an attempt to win over those who had worshipped the older gods. The monolith named the village where it stands.

Rudston, a few miles inland from Bridlington, comes from the Old English words "rood", meaning "cross" and "stan", which means "stone". There is a metal cap on the monolith now, as there has been since 1773. It protects the scar that goes back hundreds of years before that. The "rood" most probably was a crucifix attached to the head of the stone – and may have chopped three feet off its height – to persuade the worshippers of the old religion that they should embrace the new. **AV**

SAUCE

It's said Peter Stringfellow refuses to eat a cooked breakfast without it. Sean Bean had some shipped out to India when he was playing soldier Richard Sharpe from Bernard Cornwell's novels. It seems that for the sons of Sheffield, a day without Henderson's Relish is a day without sunshine. The product is South Yorkshire's answer to Worcester Sauce, introduced by a Henry Henderson at the back end of the 19th century. He cooked it up at 35 Broad Lane, Sheffield, and the bottles are still being filled, no more than a quick shake from the original site. **MH**

SAUCY

Younger people can't be bothered to write seaside postcards, spurning them to text friends and family instead. So what of that holiday pastime of browsing racks of saucy pictures which once defined the seaside experience? Their cheerful smut would show a scene such as this: a judge grills a spiv standing in the dock as a busty brunette pouts provocatively across the courtroom. "Have you ever slept with this woman?" "No, your honour, not a blooming wink!" The characters are a familiar gallery – balding, pop-eyed men intimidated by wives wielding rolling pins, nudists and

newlyweds. There are only two types of women – big-bosomed, denoting single, or big-bottomed, signalling married. It's a gleeefully sexist, size-ist, age-ist world untroubled by political correctness where nods and winks towards surreptitious sex abound. The world's biggest collection of these postcards, 20,000 or more, are not at the seaside but in an archive in Huddersfield at the Tolson Memorial Museum. They go back to 1870 when Bamforth's, probably the best-known card publishers, started in Holmfirth. A Leeds businessman took over the brand name in recent times and reckons there's plenty of life left in it yet, missus. **GH**

SEAGULLS

The humble seagull is generally regarded more fondly by visitors than residents, on whose roofs it deposits unwanted decorations. On the Yorkshire coast most are herring gulls, common gulls or the greater black-backed gull. Once huge flocks following the boats home, diving for scraps as the fishermen gutted their catch on the way into harbour, but since the demise of the east coast fleet, such a sight is rarer. But the gull is an adaptable bird, and generations of holidaymakers can attest to its fondness for chips, scraps of batter, waffles, or ice cream cones. They have learned to co-exist with the

A Bamforth Postcard from the 1980's.

changing face of coastal life from fishing to tourism, and those beady eyes often have plenty of experience behind them. Gulls can be very long-lived, the oldest ringed bird survived until the age of 31. **AV**

SHAMBLES

York has lifted the title of Europe's top city destination. This excited the people who promote the city so much their hyperbole went off the scale. Among their claims are these: Micklegate Bar equates to the Arc de Triomphe and St Mary's Abbey compares with the Coliseum. Daftest of all is a parallel they draw between the Shambles and shopping in Milan. Originally the Shambles was the noisome, poky street where the butchery businesses and allied offal-processing trades were centred. The stink must have been terrible when the most celebrated of all butchers' wives lived here. St Margaret Clitheroe married her husband in 1571 and opened her home to fugitive priests and a Catholic schoolteacher. The house she left for the last time in 1586, to be executed by crushing as punishment for her defiance, is still there to be visited. Commercially the word on the street today is uncertainty. Some shopkeepers have been squealing that the quaint medieval thoroughfare is not the tourist honeypot it once was. Caught in a squeeze of falling visitor numbers and rent rises by their landlord, York council, they have shipped out. This might bring the result of reducing souvenir shops and producing a Shambles that offers a more normal retail therapy experience. Although it's not Milan, it does possess an Italian bread shop that is worth the journey on its own. **MH**

PERCY SHAW

Asked to choose the best examples of British design in the 20th century, Concorde came top and the Spitfire second in a public poll. Receiving an honorable mention in the top 25 were catseyes – an invention whose assets are the reverse of the two winners. Percy Shaw's brilliant idea have a low profile but high utility. Halifax-born Percy was one of 14 children whose father, Jimmy, a dyer's labourer, struggled to support them all on a £1 weekly wage. Percy left school at 13 and soon had his own business repairing roads and paths with a mechanical roller he fashioned from an old Ford engine and three lorry wheels. The story goes that one foggy night in 1933 he was driving back home in Boothtown from Bradford when he hit an unlit and tricky stretch of road with a sheer drop down a hillside. He invented a flexible rubber moulding containing glass and metal beads that could be inserted at intervals down the centre of the road surface so that the reflective surfaces shone in a car's headlights. But here's the clever bit. As passing traffic depressed the moulding, the reflectors were automatically cleaned by rainwater collected in the base of the moulding. Percy's company, Reflecting Roadstuds, found orders difficult to come by until the wartime blackout arrived and his fortune was secured. Spending cash seems to have been a bigger test of Percy's invention than making it. He was not one for home comforts such as curtains and stocked his cellar with crates of his favourite Worthington's bottled beer. There were however a pair of Rolls-Royces parked in the road outside. **MH**

SHELLFISH

The great fleets that once trawled for cod, haddock and herring declined in the face of dwindling stocks and crippling quotas. The future for the ports that defined the coast and its way of life looked bleak. To the rescue came crab and lobster. The North Sea is richly stocked with both. Bridlington is now Britain's biggest shellfish port and the trade is healthy from Whitby to Withernsea. There are more than 70 boats, known as "potters", plying the waters up to 12 miles out, laying more than 70,000 of the distinctive crab and lobster pots that have become such a feature of the harbours when piled up to dry on the jetties. They gather in about 1,000 tonnes of crab a year, plus a similar weight in lobsters, and the shellfish are sent around the world, as well as ending up on the stalls that are such a well-loved feature of the seaside. Changing tastes have also done the Yorkshire fleet a favour. Amid worries about diets that contain too much salt, fat and cholesterol, shellfish is a healthy choice. Celebrity chefs Gordon Ramsay and Anthony Worral Thompson sing its praises. That can only be good news for the fishermen, and for the ports that have found a new living in waters that once seemed to offer only despair. **AV**

SHORT FAT HAIRY LEGS

He came from Leeds and in a long-running gag he was cast as the wordsmith in the Morecambe and Wise partnership. In truth, Eric was the literary one with a book on fishing and a novel to his credit and another left unfinished when he died. Ernie said at the funeral, it was "like the final curtain on one of the plays what I wrote." Death sundered a a 43-year partnership which began life on the halls in old time variety and seemed to have ended with the advent of television. After watching one of their first TV shows, the influential critic of the *Daily Mail* wrote: 'Definition of the week – TV set: a box in which they buried Morecambe and Wise'. Eric kept the cutting in his wallet for years. The television shows they went on to make, especially those with Eddie Braben's scripts, entered into legend and without those two to bring us sunshine, Christmas Day has never been quite the same. Thames Television did find a solo job for Ernie, then in his sixties, on daytime television, but it was tough trying to make it on his own. His indulgences were eating out and his Rolls Royce. Someone also made another definition – eternity was waiting for Ernie Wise to buy a round of drinks. But his comic timing was impeccable and he was the perfect foil to the one of the greatest clowns we've ever had. **MH**

SIGNS OF THE TIMES

The village of South Milford near Selby, has 45 road signs of all types in the space of half a mile. That is more rural highway clutter than anywhere else in the country. In fact it's twice as bad as the second worst, a rural road in Hampshire. North Yorkshire County Council says said the signs are there for safety reasons. Villagers want a clear-out because they reckon the signs are distracting. **GH**

SONG OF SUMMER

In 1968 Ken Russell brought Frederick Delius to a new audience when he made a film called *Song of Summer* for the BBC's culture show, *Monitor*. It was based on a 1936 memoir *Delius As I Knew Him* by Eric Fenby who had left Scarborough for the South of France to help Delius complete the

Curry invasion circa 1964.

unfinished scores he could hear in his head. Bradford-born Delius could no longer write them down because he was blind and paralysed from syphilis. Max Adrian played the bullying but brilliant Delius and Christopher Gable in his first acting role played young Eric. Born Fritz Delius in Bradford in 1862 to parents who had emigrated from Germany, he persuaded his wool merchant father to let him try his hand at cultivating oranges in Florida. Tasmin Little, one of the world's leading violinists and Delius interpreters, has dug into this part of the composer's early life and discovered a guilty secret. On the orange plantation, Solano Grove, Delius had an affair with, and then deserted, a black woman who bore him a child. **MH**

SPICY

Yorkshire's curry invasion came with the mill workers, who settled in Bradford in the 1960s. Mostly they were from Bangladesh, and from the northerly region around Pakistani Kashmir. Never mind, 'having an Indian' still means having a curry. The newcomers (always men, the women were at home) set up meeting places where the chaps could chill, chat, and eat pakora and samosa, daal and biryani, rice and unleavened flat breads such as roti. The Sweet Centre on Lumb Lane is said to be the forerunner, operating from 1964. Another early starter was the Karachi Social Club, across town. This cheap food could be dire, sometimes dazzling, usually at least interesting. Selecting "the best" curry is an idle fascination. It is as vain as choosing the best pork pie or the best pint of beer. In the 1990s the cheap curry cafe was joined by the equivalent of haute cuisine. The Aagrah chain (at the beginning a mobile stall selling to late-nighters in Shipley) brought us the more eloquent use of spices, in a smart setting, but still at an affordable price. It has a central kitchen, from where the principal ingredients are sent to its satellite restaurants. The boutique vegetarian spin-offs are rare. The most eminent at the moment is Prashad. Its long-established counterpart in Leeds is Hansas. Each serves food that is unlike the "curry" revered by the crowd at closing time. Interesting, both are owned and run by women. The subtler use of ingredients and the composition, which rarely looks like "a curry", open the mind and the taste buds.
FM

SUTTON-UNDER-WHITESTONECLIFFE

As beautiful, highly-individual Yorkshire villages go, they don't get any better than this – even when you can't see the cliff itself because of the rain. Sutton has several claims to fame, perhaps the best-known being that, with 27 letters, it comprises the longest village name in England. But there is much more than that, not least in that heartbeat of any outpost of civilisation, the local. The family expert rates the chips at the village pub as the best, absolutely anywhere. Those of us with less knowledge of these things were happy on one visit to while away Sunday lunchtime in conversation with one of the regulars, Niall Quinn, then a mere striker for Sunderland, now the chairman. Sutton is the perfect place to call on the top way to Scarborough or if heading for Whitby, Robin Hood's Bay or, finest of all, Staithes, and it is also a convenient break on the way to or from Helmsley, Hovingham or Castle Howard. It is a delight for race-goers, Thirsk being just three miles away and the stables of top trainers Kevin Ryan and Bryan Smart at the top of nearby Sutton Bank on the time-honoured turf of the Hambleton Hills. Admire the beautifully kept gardens, the white and pink wash of the houses, the ancient trees; the feeling of, well, content, is omnipresent. If you can't relax here you really can't be trying. **BB**

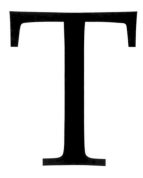

TEA

The centre of Ian Brabbin's tea world is Harrogate. The head of tea at Taylors and his small team of tasters sup about 400 samples a day, sent by producers from 40-odd countries, including China, India, Malawi, Rwanda and Sri Lanka. They still call the latter Ceylon which indicates this is a business that does not welcome too much change. Each sample has its own numbered tin box and ledgers record the results of tastings, the details of each new blend and confirmation that it has reached the standard of the previous batch. It takes some time to educate a palate. A tea tasting apprentice starts by putting the kettle on and five years later is expected to know all the ins and outs of tasting and blending. Black teas are fermented, green teas – a recent growth area – are put in an oven to dry. Our average national daily consumption is just under three cups and those who would not want to face a day without it – black or green – have been cheered by scientists' reading of the tea leaves. They have concluded a nice cup of tea, is healthy and not dehydrating, despite the caffeine. Three to four cups a day can cut the chances of heart attack and there are potential preventative cancer benefits. **GH**

TEXTILES

When the 19th century dawned, Bradford was a market town of 16,000 people and those who made a living out of wool spinning and cloth weaving did it at home. The speed and completeness of the transformation that followed is probably unequalled. By 1841 there were 108 worsted mills in the area and Bradford was set to become the wool capital of the world. Harry Franz reported it in its glory and decline. Harry, a contemporary of JB Priestley, was born in Bradford in 1912 when it was said only London's streets had more Rolls Royces. In the 1960s the Yorkshire Post made him wool textile correspondent – still a big job on the newspaper in those days – and his beat was the Bradford Wool Exchange where market day, Monday and Thursday afternoons, was attended by several hundred trading worsted tops and noils (waste removed during combing and used for heavier goods like carpets.) The Bradford Club was close by, ready to accommodate the needs of a settled caste where sons followed fathers into the business and daughters often married other woolmen's sons. Leeds too was built on wool. Richard Booth started out as early as the mid-1500s, leasing 'Armley Millnes' from Henry Saville. Shifting the stuff, over packhouse trails, was much improved when Hull was opened up by the

Tea tasting.

Aire and Calder Navigation in 1690, and routes to the west and the Atlantic trade by the Leeds-Liverpool Canal. By the mid-1800s, Leeds had 106 woollen mills, employing 10,000. As the Empire advanced and expanses of the globe were coloured red, limitless captive export markets beckoned. The end of colonialism reversed the commercial tide. Post-war, a flood of imports from hungry textile businesses in the Far East spelt the end for cheap Yorkshire mass-market goods. Richard Booth's Armley Mills succumbed and was turned into a museum in the early 1990s, many others were flattened. The surviving monuments to industrialism, where cramped generations had once sweated and slaved, were re-invented as expensive apartments, with minimalist decor, for a new breed of cool city-dweller. **MH**

THACKRAY, JAKE

A long faced, lugubrious-looking man, guitar in hand and sitting on a stool as he sings idiosyncratic ballads in a thickish Yorkshire accent, doesn't fall naturally into the category of unmissable entertainment. But with a blade-like wit and an affectionate but piercing sense of the absurd – all wrapped in the bitter sweet lyrics of life – Jake Thackray became a cult singer-songwriter and made the implausible characters of his unique world utterly believable: *Sister Josephine*, the "bloody funny nun" who is actually the burglar Big Bad Norman holed up in a convent after 15 years on the run; the engaged couple in *Lah-Di-dah* preparing for "the eyewash, all of the fancy pantomime" of what's to come; the motor-mouth wife of *On Again! On Again!* who "will never use three or four words when a couple of thousand will easily do!". The humour and bite disguised, often deliberately, his perceptive observations on love, longing and sex, his ridiculing of the class system and the pompously self-important, religion (he was devoutly Roman Catholic) and coping with everyday sadnesses or setbacks. In fact, his work was the embodiment of the adage: "Many a true word is said in jest". Thackray became a teacher in Leeds, performing in pubs and clubs before breaking into television in the 1960s, most notably on *The Frost Report*, *The Braden Beat* and *That's Life!* He disliked fuss or flummery and preferred a small stage or the corner of an intimate hall to the hot lights and cameras of a TV studio. In his own words, he didn't enjoy being a "performing dick". He even avoided the bother of an encore. "That was my last song," he'd say to an audience disarmingly " . . . and I'm going to do three more". Self-effacingly, Thackray would always wonder why people would hand over "good money" to hear him. As well as his songs, he wrote a hugely entertaining column in the *Yorkshire Post*, embraced "all things" Yorkshire and admired George Brassens and the chansonniers, with whom he was much more than favourably compared. He died on Christmas Eve in 2002, aged 63, in Monmouth, where he lived in semi-retirement after a series of financial and artistic reversals. **DH**

THIS SPORTING LIFE

A feeling of 'Yorkshireness' is relatively recent, according to historian Professor David Hey of Sheffield University. Most people had no great regional sense of belonging. Dalesmen felt nothing in common with Holderness farmers, the cutlers of Hallamshire had little enough contact with textile workers north of the Don and Dearne - never mind those living in the other two ridings. It was organised sport which changed perceptions. Sheffield's cricket ground at Bramall Lane opened in 1854 and once Yorkshire County Cricket Club got going in 1863 people hungered to identify with success. Lord Hawke and his team duly delivered, saluted county champions five times before the turn of the century. Another 27 titles followed. Five years after the last one, when the sight of the championship pennant flying at Headingley seemed a distant prospect, a Barnsley chap who had departed in 2004 to play for Essex – and had last caught the public's eye by winning Strictly Come Dacing – took charge on the pitch. Title ambitions and Yorkshire fervour were renewed. Is there a region in the country quite so sports-mad as this? Sheffield Football Club even invented the rules of our national game, although in this arena the petals have wilted on the white rose. Middlesbrough alone survives at the top level. Mighty Leeds United have been eclipsed. Green shoots of hope are there, but it requires a trip to unfashionable football parts such as Scunthorpe to find them. Fans may chant "Yorkshire! Yorkshire!" – but only when the opposition comes from outside the Broad Acres. Local rivalries and historic domestic hatreds outweigh a common identification with 'Yorkshireness'. **MH**

THREE PEAKS

You can walk them, run them and even bike them, but whichever form of transport you take, tackling the imposing edifices of Whernside (2,416ft), Ingleborough (2,373ft) and Penyghent (2,276ft) is no easy task. They sit surrounded by glorious countryside and attract hundreds of thousands of visitors every year. Many are content to just sit and look at the magnificence; others tackle a single peak and go home sated, but there are those who want more. A challenge walk over the 24 miles that encompasses this trio of Yorkshire beauties allows you 12 hours – half a day to sample the ups and downs, the highs and lows and all the wet bits in between, with (hopefully) stunning views of some of Yorkshire's finest acres. The Three Peaks may not be mountains, but they are not to be taken lightly. And if you think 12 hours is not a long time to traverse those 24 miles, the record-holder for the famous Three Peaks fell race, held every April, is Andy Peace, of Bingley Harriers. He once got round the course in 2 hours 46 minutes and three seconds. And to prove we're not sexist, the women's record is 3 hours 16 minutes and 17 seconds and is held by Sarah Rowell. **DO**

TIME LORD

John Harrison

It's hard to overstate John Harrison's significance. At out-of-the-way Barton-on-Humber, he changed the course of history by inventing marine clocks that were accurate. These proto-chronometers revolutionised navigation by allowing captains to get a fix on their ships' longitude and gave Britannia mastery of the waves. Until then, mariners out of sight of land had been able to work out their latitude by measuring the height of the sun or stars. But failure to crack the longitude question led to such a loss of lives and ships that all merchantile nations were ready to throw money at anyone who reckoned they had solved it. The British government offered the biggest cash prize of all in 1714. The physics were straightforward. Since the Earth rotates by 15 degrees an hour, a two-hour time-difference would represent 30 degrees of longitude. So if the local time is 10am on a ship and noon at Greenwich, the navigator knows he is 30 degrees west of Greenwich. But the practicalities of keeping time accurately at sea defeated everyone until Harrison, a carpenter by trade, came along and eventually collected his due full reward in 1773. **MH**

TOT LORD

One thing lacking as the years pass is the person known as "a character". Sometimes they are eccentric, sometimes crazy, sometimes forthright, sometimes you don't quite know what it is. These are not famous people but "locals". What they have in common is that they stand out. Hannah Hauxwell was a character, which is why she became famous for her detached existence on a hill farm. Tot Lord was a character. This

Penyghent and Whernside, Ribblesdale. Bruce Rollinson.

Sue Everatt holds the replica H4 first created by John Harrison.

sturdy Dalesman lived in and around Settle, in the West Riding of Yorkshire and was an amateur historian, explorer, caver, man of property. He was born at the end of the 19th century and served in the 1914–18 as a boy soldier, enlisting under-age. He was a pioneer with the Craven Pothole Club and a warden on the formation of the Cave Rescue Organisation. In the 1920s and 1930s he was exploring caves in the limestone behind Settle in the company of other inquisitive

men who became known as the Settle Pig Yard Club. Their early finds were kept in old pig sties. Between 1921 and 1926 he made discoveries in Attermire Cave and eventually visited and developed our knowledge of the neolithic animals and men who had lived or sheltered in the districts caves, such as Albert, Jubilee and Victoria. The latter revealed worked flints, bronze age pots and a range of animal bones. Tot Lord (he never used his name Thomas) moved to Town

Head, a large house on the edge of Settle, in 1948 and here he exhibited many of the cave finds in what was called the Pig Yard Museum. He dug out a cellar for further exhibit space. He made the display cases for thousands of specimens. In the 1950s he was a feisty member of Settle Rural District Council and spoke his mind. Of the newly-formed Yorkshire Dales National Park he asked, "What do these people sitting in front of their fires in Leeds know about the needs of Dales people?" On the town's dirty streets, he opined that the authorities were waiting for the weather to break and a good downpour to clear the gutter of paper and rubbish. He died in 1965. His house was demolished in the 1970s. He is remembered by the Tot Lord Trail, a walk through the woods in the grounds of his old home, and in the work of the Tot Lord Trust. His explorations are described in Tot Lord and the Bone Caves by WR Mitchell, chronicler of the region and its people. He died aged 65 in 1965. His family carry on this interest in nature. **FM**

TREES

Trees are precious. Their growth absorbs carbon from the atmosphere and is a natural measure against global warming. The forest floor encourages unique plant and insect life and the branches and seeds are both a home and a meal for birds. Landowners receive grants to plant ghylls with bird-friendly species, such as alder and the berry-rich rowan. The Yorkshire Dales Millennium Trust is spending £672,000 on the Dales woodland restoration, planting 370 acres. The arboretum at Thorp Perrow, near Bedale, was started in the 1930s by the shipping magnate Sir Leonard Ropner and the 85-acre wooded wonderland rates as one of the nation's finest. Castle Howard has oak trees that are 500 years old and there's an arboretum, run with the Royal Botanical Gardens at Kew. This year the Woodland Trust launched its search for the country's oldest trees and one of them is the Laund Oak on the Bolton Abbey estate. Over 800 years old, it's thought to have been named after John of Laund, the Prior from 1286 to 1330 and marked the point where the Forests of Barden and Knaresborough met. Nearby, along the banks of the Wharfe, is the epitome of mixed ancient woodland, known as Strid Woods. Birdsong, sylvan vistas and an array of flora greet the visitor. A perfect place to find a green thought in a green shade. **FM**

TUNES OF GLORY

As recently as 1991, 19 of the Grimethorpe band's 27 players were pitmen. The pit shut the following year. Today's band players no longer need to be card-carrying members of the working class. All but one are "outsiders" – teachers, accountants, mechanics, university technicians – who commute to twice-weekly rehearsals from as far as Hull and Birmingham. It has not changed the sound. Elgar Howarth, the conductor who broadened Grimethorpe's scope with commissions from contemporary composers, described it as craggy, dark, and throaty. It's said only three brass bands can fill any hall in Britain, all from Yorkshire – Grimethorpe, Brighouse and Rastrick and Black Dyke (John Foster's mills at Queensbury which brought that band into existence closed many years ago). Grimethorpe found fame in the wider world thanks to its role in the film *Brassed Off* which presented banding as a potent symbol of a coalfield culture that was passing away. **GH**

Grimethorpe Colliery Band

TURNER'S YORKSHIRE

The light, the moors and the 'monuments of antiquity' in Yorkshire time and again tempted JMW Turner northwards. The finest watercolourist of his, or any other, age relished as only an artist properly can the cut and colour of its stone and the fact that the capaciousness of its weather constantly 're-created' the landscape. Shape and shade were fluid, and forever changing, and Turner was obliged to use his skill to keep up or just to 'imagine' what he saw (his interpretations are, of course, integral to his genius).John Ruskin, the most astute of critics, thought Yorkshire was Turner's inspiration, where he found "great solemnity and simplicity of subject" and produced detail that was "exquisitely delicate".

The paintings and drawings also prove Ruskin wholly correct in his assessment that no one but Turner could so "stirringly and truthfully measure the moods of Nature". His debt to Yorkshire began as soon as he arrived in it, aged 22, for the first time in 1797. The fierce beauty of the place enthralled him. After a commission to draw scenes of Sheffield and Wakefield was out of the way, Turner soon explored far further afield, gladly swapping urban for rural, and feverishly sketched churches and abbeys, such as Kirstall and Fountains. The poetic

element of this work won him associateship of the Royal Academy.

A friendship in Yorkshire was pivotal to his life. He found an admirer and confidant in Walter Fawkes, an MP and fairly wealthy landowner, who inherited Farnley Hall near Leeds. The house was part Jacobean, part late 18th century. Turner, given his own suite of rooms, visited regularly, usually during the summer or autumn, and rode out on prodigious sketching and painting tours (some experimental) across the Dales and around the coast. During one of them Turner wrote: "weather miserably wet; I shall be web-foot, like a Drake – excepting the curled feather . . ."

Fawkes was an inveterate Turner collector, exhibited his paintings in London and even figured in some of them himself, such as *Frosty Morning* (1813) and *Grouse Shooting on Beamsley Beacon* (1816). After his patron died in 1825, Turner never returned to Farnley Hall. "My good Auld lang sine is gone," he said. Turner abandoned, and eventually gave away, a sketchbook he had been using shortly before Fawkes' death because it reminded him of his terrible grief. Yorkshire, however, always stayed with him. **DH**

UGANDAN

Archbishop Sentamu

It's said the Church of England survived because it had shrewdly judged how much religion the English would take – which was not very much. These days the gods that stand tallest are celebrity and shopping. In their shadow, princes of the the church tend to wring their hands and sigh about the multitudes worshipping in the temples of materialism. Dr John Sentamu does neither. The Archbishop's direct speaking contrasts with the usually opaque sentiments of top churchmen. He believes in getting out and about and connects with ordinary people and their concerns. If he thinks he sees an opportunity to change things he seizes it – such as posting to MPs copies of a 100-Minute Bible entitled *Do Nothing to Change Your Life*. This includes a plea for the nation to ditch endless "to do" lists, non-stop emails and the 24/7 culture. Britain's first black archbishop was born near Kampala, in Uganda, in 1949, the sixth of 13 children. As a judge in the Uganda High Court in 1974, he dared confront President Idi Amin's brutal regime and was beaten up and jailed for his pains. He's a long-standing football fan, Manchester United having captured his heart 40 years ago when they toured Uganda. Now he is also the patron of York City and a regular in the stand at Kit Kat Crescent, a place that has sorely tested the faith of those who also attend, week-in, week-out, for a very long time. **MH**

UMPIRE

Nothing better conveys his popularity, or the esteem and affection in which he is held, than the straightforward fact that Harold Dennis Bird – born the son of a coalminer on April 19, 1933 in Barnsley – became known to everyone who watched cricket, and even to the vast proportion of those who didn't, as plain 'Dickie'. To be instantly recognised merely by your nickname is one of the definitions of celebrity. To hear it expressed so warmly by total strangers, as if you actually belong to their family, is a compliment bestowed on very few people. But then he was uncommonly good at his job. In an umpiring career that stretched from 1969 to 1996, and embraced 66 Tests and three World Cup finals, he belonged to the rarest of breeds; in fact, many might argue it remains a species of one – a sports official who simultaneously inspired admiration, trust and respect among players and the cricket public. Most of all, he was – and continues to be – immensely well liked and utterly devoted to cricket.

Archbishop John Sentamu.

Lindis Percy and Alan Bennett at Menwith Hill.

As a player, he scored an unbeaten 181 for Yorkshire at Glamorgan at Bradford Park Avenue. Such was the formidable competition for places in the team – it was 1959, after all – that he was unstrapping his pads in the dressing room when the selectors dropped him. Frustration eventually led him to Leicestershire, a move he confessed as the "biggest mistake of my career." He retired prematurely from the first class game, aged 32. When umpiring beckoned, he soon established himself as its master practitioner, as scrupulously honest in his decision-making as an Appeal Court judge, and with the disarming knack of talking to players rather than at them without diminishing his authority. From Lillee to Botham, from Sobers to Richards, he was "the best". There were endearing foibles and idiosyncrasies: the twitches and stretches, the awful fear of arriving late which meant he turned up everywhere with hours to spare. There were always incidents to busy him: bomb scares (so he sat on the covers), burst pipes, the reflection from car windscreens, and the constant threat of bad light. And there were the pleasurable highs of success: an MBE, a guard of honour and standing ovation for his final Test at Lord's and a best selling autobiography in which Michael Parkinson encapsulated him perfectly. "Only Shakespeare," he said. "could have invented a character so full of life's rich juices". **DH**

UNCLE SAM IN YORKSHIRE

Legions of excellent Polish plumbers, electricians and bricklayers have already voted with their feet. They prefer the rewards here to what's available back home where an odd couple, identical twins Lech and

Jaroslaw Kaczynski, are making a mess of things. Respectively Poland's president and prime minister, the Kaczynskis have thumbed their noses at Moscow by inviting George Bush to install missiles on Polish territory in President Putin's backyard. As the Kremlin flexes its muscles, the Americans look again at their protective cover where Yorkshire plays a key role. Conveniently, at RAF Fylingdales on the North York moors, the Americans have just paid £400m for an upgrade. Since 1963 Fylingdales has looked east, ready with a four-minute warning of Armageddon. Expect nothing as leisurely from the new improved version whose warning of an incoming nuclear strike will be seconds not minutes. The Americans have also just beefed-up their listening station at Menwith Hill, near Harrogate. This also is only nominally an RAF station and has now become part of America's missile defence shield. This move did not impress Yorkshire protestor Lindis Percy, co-founder of the Campaign for the Accountability of American Bases. Lindis, Britain's best-known peacenik, has been arrested more often than she can remember, been jailed over a dozen times and is banned from five US bases, including her local Menwith Hill. She has some high-profile support. For her July 4 Freedom from America demonstration in 2007, Lindis was joined at Menwith Hill by Yorkshire's greatest literary treasure, Alan Bennett. **MH**

UP AND UNDER

Rugby League

It all began at a meeting at the George Hotel in Huddersfield in 1995 attended by Rupert Murdoch, Maurice Lindsay and Lord Voldemort, who between them invented a whole new sport to provide a bit of padding between the unrelenting football coverage on satellite television. Or at least that's what many of the followers of the clubs that failed to make it into the bright new world of Super League in 1996 will tell you. The sport did secure £87m to ease the passage from winter to summer but the 'broken heart' payments received by the likes of Keighley and Featherstone were accepted only grudgingly. A hundred years before, the Northern working class rugby union clubs had split from the snooty RFU to form their own competition in a row over broken-time payments. Over the course of the next century the Northern Union evolved into rugby league, losing two players, developing a healthy chip on its shoulder and re-writing the rule book to become much more than merely a version of rugby union with all the boring bits removed. Down the years rugby league has also enriched the English language with terms such as 'gerremonside,' 'early bath' and 'up and under,' the latter two phrases being inventions of TV commentator Eddie Waring, a man villified by many Northerners for having the temerity to try and popularise the game. **JL**

UTOPIA: SALTAIRE

It wasn't new for an industrialist to dream of an ideal community for his workers. Half a century before Titus Salt created Saltaire, Robert Owen led the way in Scotland. Owen bought four textile factories in New Lanark and put into practice his belief that given the right working and living conditions, people were perfectable. This was a period when it was acceptable for five-year-olds to work for 13 hours a day in a mill, so Owen had a long way to go. Bradford, as it surged forward as the wool capital of the world, was a hell-hole for the casualties of the factory system, the sweated workforce. Titus Salt looked to a green-field site four miles out of town where

Menwith Hill

he could try out his own advanced ideas. Two architects, Lockwood and Mawson, constructed for him a mill that looked like the palace of an Italian Renaissance prince, but much bigger. More modest in construction, but no less vital to Salt's plan, were the rows of solid, decent houses for his employees, with a school, hospital, churches, Sunday school, washhouse, shops and no pubs. Saltaire was a "a paradise on the sylvan banks of the Aire, far from the stench and vice of the industrial city".

Launched in the high tide of Victorian prosperity, Titus Salt's vast mill lay beached and useless by the seventh decade of the 20th century. Council efforts to re-animate it had failed. It needed someone with the energy and imagination of the founder could bring this back to life. Step forward Jonathan Silver, a man with a mission to forge art and commerce into a powerful lever to open the immense potential of a place which seemed an embarrassing anachronism. Silver pursued his goal assisted by a gift for making headlines and his friendship with David Hockney. Saltaire is now a World Heritage Site, visited by over 750,000 people a year. It's popularity comes at a price. Those homes built for a Victorian workers' utopia are now in private hands and a stone-built three

Saltaire

bedroom former millhands' terrace home in Saltaire now costs about £180,000. **MH**

UTTER DISGRACE

Compo

The longest-running sitcom on television almost didn't happen. When the cast was brought together for the first time, for dinner in a Huddersfield hotel, it was clear that two of them didn't see eye-to-eye. Bill Owen had strong socialist convictions and Michael Bates (Blamire, the original ringleader of this band of whimsical duffers living out a second childhood) was true blue. When they got onto the issue of Mrs Thatcher, right or wrong, things became so heated the producer had to take the pair of them outside. He told them in no uncertain terms that the script they had from Roy Clarke was a winner and they could not allow political differences to jeopardise things. A truce was agreed. It did not need to hold for too long because Michael Bates quit after the second series for health reasons and died not long afterwards. Compo, gap-toothed and stubble-cheeked under his trademark woolly hat, continued to steal the show as the perennial adolescent, easily led in his turned-over wellies, into dodgy escapades. His most treasured plans concerned what he would like to do to Nora Batty. To everyone else, a scary, wrinkled-stocked harpie, Nora was, in Compo's lustful eyes, a buxom sex-bomb, a Sophia Loren of the Yorkshire Pennines. His urges were so urgent she regularly had to resort to a flailing broom to defend her chastity. Peter Sallis, who played Clegg, says that Bill Owen invested the part with his own ideas, especially the look and reckons it was one of the finest comic characterisations of the age.

Although Bill Owen died in July 1999, advance filming meant he appeared in a special episode in January 2000, followed by a programme called *Bill Owen: A Tribute*. The first three of the ten episodes for the 21st *Last of the Summer Wine* series had also been completed. Roy Clarke re-wrote the remaining seven and included Compo's death with a funeral much like the one in real life a few months earlier. Replacing Compo was his long-lost son Tom, played by Tom, Bill Owen's son. **MH**

Ribblehead viaduct

Janet's Foss, near Gordale
Scar in Malhamdale.

WHITELEY, RICHARD

He used to joke that when he died, the *Yorkshire Post* would run the headline: "Ferret Man Dies". That was a reference to the much-repeated moment in 1977 when a ferret clamped its jaws around his forefinger on camera in *Calendar* and refused to let go. And when he did die, much too young at 61, in June 2005 it was testament to the affection in which Richard Whiteley was held by the public that they thought of him with a smile, not least because of the ferret. There was no gulf between the affable Whiteley they saw on screen and the man off it. His was a genuine, unaffected warmth, and no other television presenter from Yorkshire has quite held the place in viewers' hearts.

Born in Bradford, educated at Giggleswick, making his home in the Dales, Whiteley barely left the Broad Acres apart from his time at Cambridge, where he took,

by his own admission "a crappy Third" in English. That was typically self-deprecating. He was an exceptionally intelligent man, who was snapped up by the ITN graduate scheme and joined the fledgling Yorkshire Television in 1965 as a reporter. Three years later, he was present at the opening night of *Calendar*. Whiteley was a fine journalist, and notable triumphs included being the first to interview Margaret Thatcher after the Brighton bombing in 1984. *Countdown* was only meant to have a short run when it opened Channel 4 in 1982, but 23 years later it was still going strong, by which time Whiteley had clocked up more time on television than anyone else alive apart from the girl on the test card. His rapport with co-presenter Carol Vorderman, his 200-plus garish jackets, 500-plus loud ties, and awful puns made the show a hit. Whiteley's took a one-man show to the Edinburgh Festival, was named Yorkshire Man of the Year in 2003, and the following year received the OBE. He devoted himself to numerous good causes in Yorkshire and to the end downplayed how good he was, saying of *Countdown*: "I'm not a natural quiz show host. If I had to apply for my own job today, I wouldn't get it." **AV**

WILBERFORCE, WILLIAM

Wilberforce is alive and well and living near Wetherby. A direct descendant of the Hull MP, he is an accountant who also manages the family estate. Inevitably he took an unaccustomed spotlight in the year that marked the 200th anniversary of the Abolition of Slavery Act. The original Wilberforce succeeded because his moral commitment was allied to extraordinary Parliamentary tenacity and physical courage. At one point, he could not enter Liverpool for fear for his life. A similar impulse led him to press for laws to end child labour. Here employers took a similar line to the slavers – arguing for its continuance in the name of national wealth-creation. There are dissenters at the Wilberforce shrine. Although he was the catalyst for the British ban, the transatlantic slave trade horrors continued until the 1830s. Some think Wilberforce receives too much credit for a battle that was fought by many – most importantly, by the slaves themselves. There's also a feeling that the large wads of lottery cash that paid for the 200th anniversary celebrations might have been more usefully spent on inquiring into the causes of the deep disaffection among the young within Britain's present black communities. **MH**

WILD FLOWERS

Believe it or not, Yorkshire is blessed with wild flowers. You just have to look for them. Some are more obvious than others – witness the fields of blood-red poppies, the great waves of ox-eye daisies, whole glades of foxgloves, woodlands whose floors turn to moving seas of bluebells – and some are more welcome. Himalayan balsam may be pretty and long-flowering, but it is taking over huge areas of damp and shady land once the home to native, less-invasive wild flowers. Wild garlic is another rampaging plant, but it's still a delight (if somewhat of a smelly one) when in spring it clothes the ground in woodlands. Elsewhere, the Yorkshire Dales are home to many rare and beautiful orchids, and the limestone terraces of the Craven area provide ideal growing conditions for numerous small but beautiful plants. And on the east coast, the clifftops are covered by vast tracts of red campion. But wild flowers come in many forms and given a chance, will thrive. So, the reduction in the use of herbicides, particularly on roadsides, has encouraged many plants to take hold. Now it's possible to see common orchids blooming within feet of the busiest motorways. These are the obvious ones whose size and colour make them stand out. But lower down, in and among the grass, living in cracks in mortar are hundreds of wild flowers just getting on with their business of growing, seeding and increasing their numbers. Tiny cranesbills, sedums, saxifrages, bell flowers...look and you'll find them. **DO**

XS

poll-topper Harold Wilson

Huddersfield's Harold Wilson, snug in his raincoat, gently puffing his pipe and speaking in that deliberate, nasal, West Yorkshire accent, was the most successful politician of the 20th century in terms of persuading voters to put their "X" next to his party's candidates. The personal image never quite squared with facts. Despite the pipe he was a cigar smoker. The plain man's raincoat was made by Gannex, run by his eventually-to-be-jailed friend Joseph (later Lord) Kagan, at his factory in Elland. The bluff Yorkshire demeanor disguised a brilliant mind skilful at brokering deals with trades union barons in smoke-filled rooms. He led an often fractious party for 13 years and what remains in the memory are his deft one-liners – his judgment of the state of Labour's party organisation as "penny farthing"; his insistence that Britain would be transformed by the "white heat of technology"; his laying the blame for Britain's balance-of-payments crisis with "the gnomes of Zurich". Others that still echo down the years are, "the pound in your pocket"; "thirteen years of Tory misrule" ; "a week is a long time in politics" and "beer and sandwiches at No 10". His narrowest of victories in 1964 – the year after he succeeded Hugh Gaitskell as

leader – reassured those who were fearful of socialism red in tooth and showed that Labour could be the natural party of government. Harold Wilson's conviction that the Labour Party owed more to Methodism than to Marxism made him an instinctive middle-of-the-roader who was happy, by-and-large, to endorse the post-war political consensus. Significantly, he said his proudest legacy was the Open University. The bronze statue of him in Huddersfield's St George's Square, omitted the trademark pipe at the request of his wife Mary. **BB**

XEROX (AND RANK)

He was the man behind the chap who banged the gong for the Rank Organisation. J Arthur Rank came from a rich Hull flour-milling family, although his early prospects did not look too bright in the eyes of his father. He told him he was a dunce whose only way of getting on would be in the mill. The prophecy seemed self-fulfilling. When J Arthur struck out on his own – setting up a self-raising flour business – it failed. He returned to work for dad but found time to get involved with the Religious Film Society. A fervent Methodist, J Arthur was fired by the idea that cinema could put over wholesome stories and role models. He found the real celluloid world to be keen on

his money but not on his message.   Yet this principled man, a teetotaller with a strict moral outlook, rose more successfully than his flour. He bought the Odeon and Gaumont chains and by 1946, when cinema-going peaked, his organisation owned five studios. He also started the famous 'Charm School' through which flounced almost every starlet of the Fifties and early Sixties. With more than 650 cinemas, the Rank Organisation was bigger than its Hollywood rivals and J Arthur was the patron of the major creative talents of the time. Michael Powell and Emeric Pressburger, David Lean, Frank Launder and Sidney Gilliat all applauded him for being allowed to spend as much money as they needed on making Rank films. No wonder they called him Uncle Arthur. When his older brother Jimmy died in 1952, J Arthur went back to the family flour business. In 1956, Rank offered to bankroll the struggling Haloid company in America, which pioneered Xerox duplicating machines, in return for rights to make and market them. Inside ten years, Rank Xerox was making a third of the organisation's profits. Footnote: the man who banged the Rank gong as the cinemas curtains parted was Ken Richmond – a 19 stone, 6ft 5ins, a wrestler, boxer, judo enthusiast and Jehovah's Witness. **MH**

PROF XAVIER

Patrick Stewart

The teen audiences who flocked to see the X Men films and cheered on the wheelchair-bound Professor Xavier in his battle with the diabolical Magneto probably had no idea that they were watching one of this country's finest classical actors. Patrick Stewart, son of Mirfield, where he was born in 1940, has a stage career going back almost 50 years. The acting bug bit early. He dropped out of Mirfield Secondary Modern School at 15, and became involved in local theatre before enrolling on a two-year acting course at the Bristol Old Vic Theatre School. Stewart's trademark bald pate had developed by the age of 19, and he tells the story of how friends held him down and shaved off his remaining hair. With true Yorkshire grit, Stewart made a virtue out of his baldness, auditioning with and without a wig and telling producers that they were getting two actors for the price of one. His Yorkshire connections remain strong – he is Chancellor of Huddersfield University, and frequently turns up to watch Huddersfield Town. Prof Xavier and Capt Jean-Luc Picard in Star Trek: The Next Generation, made him wealthy and famous. He has recently returned to the Shakespearean fold, receiving rave reviews for his performances in The Tempest and Antony and Cleopatra. AV

XSCAPE

Junction 32 of the M62 offers an exit from economic failure for the parts around Normanton and Castleford. Historically locked into the coal industry, the area's new route to progress involves going down hill at speed. Opened in autumn 2003, Xscape offers the country's biggest indoor snow slope. It's good for beginners and it does have the novelty of being proper snow. Looming beside the motorway, Xscape also has rock-climbing walls, an aerial assault course, skateboard park, bowling, cinemas, bars, restaurants and shops. Initially this may have seemed a strange road to take towards economic regeneration, especially as the man taking the wheel was PY Gerbeau. This is the former captain of the French Olympic ice hockey team who was recruited from Euro Disney to turn round the Millennium Dome in Greenwich. He's now head of X-Leisure, the biggest leisure-property company in the country, and things seem to have gone much more smoothly since he left the failure of the Dome behind. PY's most-loved book is The Art of War by the ancient Chinese strategist Sun Tzu who offers this advice in his pages: "anger may in time change to gladness; vexation may be succeeded by content." That seems to sum up the mood on the Yorkshire coalfield snow slope. **MH**

X MARKS THE SPOT

At the end of what seemed a cold and fruitless day in September in 1985, Ted Seaton's two friends, on a metal detecting expedition near Middleham Castle, switched off their machines and made their way back to the car. Ted lingered a few more moments on a bridleway that led from Jervaulx Abbey to Coverham Abbey and passed Middleham Castle – once home to Richard III. Alerted by a faint signal at the edge of a bridleway, Ted discovered, about 15 inches under the surface, what looked like a thrown-away powder compact. Later cleaning revealed the compact to be a gold pendant inset with a sapphire. The 15th century Middleham Jewel was judged not to be Treasure Trove and was bought for £1.3m at auction by an unknown foreign buyer. The Yorkshire Museum raised over £2.4m to save it for the nation. The most recent big-time Yorkshire treasure find was in a ploughed field near Harrogate. David Whelan, who is semi-retired, and his son Andrew, a surveyor, were told last month by the British Museum that the Viking hoard their metal detectors revealed – 617 silver coins, a gold arm ring and a gilt silver vessel – was of global significance. **GH**

YORK

It's Yaahk to most of the people born here, if not to the hordes who flood in. The daytime streets can be should-to-shoulder with Romans, Vikings, Cavaliers and Roundheads all dressed up to rake over the ashes of battles past. They move aside when darkness falls for girls in pink fairy wings, or very short gym slips, heading unsteadily towards where they hope the action is in the Hen Night capital of Europe. What used to get Yaahkies out of bed in the morning was chocolate and cocoa, glass-blowing, railway carriages, printing and sugar-making. Apart from the first two, they have all gone. Now it's biosciences, finance, education and tourism. And more tourism. The Castle Museum pioneered virtual reality history with their Kirkgate Victorian Street in 1938. Others followed, and this is now the second most-visited city in the kingdom where the guides on the open-top tour buses used to wave their arms at the 'layer cake of history'.

What makes York a happening tourist city is the fact that not too much happened in the past. When it was Yorkshire's workplace, the corporation failed to sort out navigation on the Ouse for coal vessels needing to improve supplies. So industrialisation happened elsewhere. Later, as other places viewed their ancient walls as a useless drag on expansion and flattened them, York

hestitated. A campaign led by a local painter, William Etty, eventually persuaded the authorities to take their favourite option. Doing nothing proved to be a winner in the long-term. The bar walls are now one of the chief glories along with the Minster, the racecourse, the Shambles, Guy Fawkes, Dick Turpin, George Hudson and the National Railway Museum, plus Dame Judi Dench. York simply can't go wrong. Or can it? By small degrees distinctiveness is surrendered. One small example: FR Stubbs, for generations an ironmonger's shop on a little cobbled bridge over the Foss, recently closed. It is now a fish restaurant, a franchise operation, just like one in Leeds and elsewhere. Uniformity is the enemy of uniqueness. The commercial pressures on York are now so intense and the visitors so numerous, it might just be lovcd to death.
MH

YORKSHIRE COTTAGE

No domestic library in Yorkshire is complete without *Yorkshire Cottage*, a book which seals forever in words and pen and ink drawings a lost and elegiac world. The story begins in 1938. Artist Marie Hartley and writer Ella Pontefract buy "a lost child of a house" – a derelict cottage called Coleshouse in Wensleydale. The cottage is "humble and

York Minster.

Marie Hartley and Ella Pontefract.

ordinary", with old beams, a stone-flagged floor, uneven stairs and a solitary cold tap. The first half of Yorkshire Cottage intricately describes its shilling-an-hour, three-year restoration into a book-lagged haven with smoke climbing in elegant vines from the chimney. The second half is a calendar capturing the essence of Dales life. There are poetic passages about winter's "glassy coatings" of snow, the birdlife, such as sandpipers, curlews and black-headed gulls, and the way the summer light falls across the wiry grass of the Fells and intensifies the colours of the flowers: cow parsley, reddish-brown sorrel, mauve meadow crane's-bill. The village blacksmith is busy (he made all the hinges and snecks for the cottage), furniture is delivered by horse drawn cart, the hay is cut by "mowing machine" and

forked into pikes, a family of potters camp benevolently on the green with a piebald horse.

Marie and Ella have an ear for dialect, an eye for nature and an appreciation of the "spare and hard-working" Dalesmen and women. No matter how many times you read the book, the effect it has on you is always the same: you long to find your own cottage in the Dales and live there exactly like Marie and Ella. When the book was published (in 1942), the exact location of cottage was never mentioned in the text. But you will find it beside the moor road in Askrigg, where readers regularly sought out it and the authors. "We never thought," wrote Marie "that anyone would take the trouble to ascertain its whereabouts. We were sadly mistaken. . . ". Ella died of chronic high blood pressure in 1945. She published six books with Marie, who also wrote Yorkshire Heritage: A Memoir to Ella Pontefract and then co-authored a further 13 titles with Joan Ingilby. She continued to live in Coleshouse until her death, aged 100, in May 2006. **DH**

YORKSHIRE CURD TART

A moist filling, not too highly seasoned with the vaguest hint of nutmeg, seedless dried fruit, pastry just turned brown but not crumbly, the top a mixture of milky white and golden brown. This, or something close to it, has been familiar in the Dales for centuries, originally as a heartening snack for hungry workers in the farmhouse or hayfield. The ingredients are shortcrust pastry, and for the filling: butter, sugar, milk curds, seedless raisins or currants, wholemeal breadcrumbs, salt, nutmeg, eggs (this from English Food by Jane Grigson, who remarked that she found most recipes too sweet). Rick Stein's recipe (in the Food Heroes television series) makes the curds overnight using

Yorkshire Curd Tart.

rennet and milk, but adds allspice — which is a seasoning too far for this tart enthusiast. The exposure on national television has spread the fame of the north country tea time treat. Some years ago in a "blind tasting" for this paper. Elijah Allen from Hawes won. For those who can't get to the Wensleydale grocers, Bettys tea shops sell an excellent curd tart. Accompany it with a cup of your favourite tea. **FM**

YORKSHIRE PARKIN

Dark and sweet and moistly chewy, with black treacle, soft brown sugar, oatmeal, and ginger (to warm the blood) – this is a mouthwatering combination. Yorkshire Parkin eaten in the light of a bonfire to celebrate a York man and his Gunpowder Plot make a great early November treat. Lighting bonfires at this time of year go back a long way before 1605 and Guy Fawkes. The Vikings had a similar idea and made 'thar cakes' for the occasion. Parkin fills you up, being one of those economical teabreads known as cut-and-come-again cakes. The treacle in the mixture caramelises and hardens during baking, so the cake is best kept for a few days for it to 'come again' – when the caramel softens and each slice has the right crumby stickiness. **GH**

YORKSHIRE PUDDING

The county is best known for Yorkshire Pudding. This humble flour batter recipe is served around the world with roast beef. Also, solo with fillings of: stew, beans, chilli, curry etc. Traditionally, and this is the way my father cooked it, the batter mix is poured into a hot baking tray already lubricated with melted fat from the beef, and cooked in a hot oven on a shelf underneath the beef, which is free to drip more fat on to the pudding. Heart-stirring stuff. The pudding was served before the beef, apparently to temper the appetite ahead of the expensive joint of beef. Well, when I was in my carnivorous youth, such was the quality of the pudding that we would often have it before the meat, and then with it. The recipe could not be simpler and whilst some may favour father's literal pudding texture with crisp edges, baked in a single tray, others like lots of air in the base of individual round puddings. Goodness knows what leads to the ghastly leathery puddings often served in restaurants and pubs. A vast industry seems to be making frozen Yorkshire puddings but for the real thing make your own. Take flour, milk and water, an egg, salt and pepper (I like a good pinch of mustard powder), combine to a smooth batter, let it stand for an hour and then cook in a baking tray in a hot oven. Ultra traditional types may use ye olden method and finish the cooking in front of an open fire. Eat with beef gravy. **FM**

YORKSHIRE WOLDS

THE Yorkshire Wolds may not be the most dramatic landscape in the Broad Acres, but they are amongst its most beautiful. The crescent of rolling hills that rise from the Humber at Hessle and curve north towards Bempton, where they soar to the majestic cliffs have a charm all of their own. This is a gentle landscape of farmland and pretty villages, and a unique one, for the Wolds are the most northerly outcrop of chalk in Britain. The soil is fertile, and farmers have grown crops here for thousands of years, the testament to their labours being found in the remains of medieval villages and burial grounds from the Neolothic, Bronze and Iron ages. The Wolds are easily forgotten by too many people in Yorkshire, who head instead

Yorkshire Pudding.

for the grandeur of the Dales, or the ruggedness of the North York Moors. The Wolds have a quieter beauty than either, and walking the 80-mile Wolds Way that runs from Hessle to Filey Brigg is the ideal way to appreciate it. So great is David Hockney's passion for the area, he now forsakes California for Bridlington from where he rushes out at every opportunity to capture Wolds nature in all its moods. Giant paintings that resulted from his forays were such a hit at the Royal Academy and Tate Britain that the local tourist board launched discounted 'Hockney Trail' holidays. Locals fear a rush of outsiders will compromise their tranquillity. **AV**

ZEPPELINS

It appeared over Hull not long after midnight on June 6 1915, and gave Yorkshire its first taste of aerial warfare. Zeppelin L9 of the German air force dropped at least 32 bombs on the city centre from 3,000ft, killing 24 people, wounding 64 and wrecking 40 houses. Firemen worked through the night to save Holy Trinity Church. People were enraged and mobs attacked a number of shops believed to have German connections. Over the next three years, Zeppelins were to put Yorkshire in the front line of the First World War. The great, slow-moving, cigar-shaped airships headed for major industrial centres, following rivers or railway lines – Middlesbrough, Scarborough, York, Wetherby, Driffield, Pontefract, and Goole were hit. They found Hull again in July 1916, when 10 people were killed, and returned on September 24 1917. By then, improved air defences had forced the airships higher to 16,000ft, reducing the accuracy of their bombing. The Zeppelins returned to Hull in March 1918, but did little damage. The worst Yorkshire toll was in Sheffield, attacked by Zeppelin L22 on the night of September 26 1916. The Burngreave and Darnall areas suffered and a memorial was set in a factory wall in the East End to commemorate the 29 people who died. **AV**

ZETLAND LIFEBOAT

The Zetland Lifeboat Museum at King Street, Redcar houses the world's oldest surviving lifeboat. The cost of building it, £200, was raised by local fishing families with a local landowner, Lord Dundas and a clergyman chipping in. The vessel arrived in Redcar on 7th October 1802 to be christened in honour of the Lord of the Manor, Lord Zetland. She was rowed out regularly into the teeth of fierce storms by local heroes of the Teesbay Lifeboat and Shipwreck Society and over 500 lives were saved. The RNLI took over in 1858, eventually commissioning a new lifeboat and ordering the Zetland be destroyed. But the sentimental ties within the fishing community were so strong the RNLI had to back down and have the Zetland repaired instead. The locals were right. When the brig Luna got into difficulties in 1880, three lifeboats had to be launched and Zetland was one of them. When she was finally retired, Lord Zetland made space in a barn at Marske. Later, a council-run lifeboat museum had a chequered history until a Save the Zetland campaign in the 1970s resulted in museum and lifeboat both being transferred to the RNLI to secure their future. **MH**

The Zetland Lifeboat Museum in Redcar houses the world's oldest surviving lifeboat. Mike Cowling

ZOO

It's certainly changed over the years since it was called the Flamingo Land Zoological Gardens. I went there on a Wallace Arnold coach at the beginning of the Sixties just after a few small fairground-style rides had been introduced. Yes, the pink flamingoes were there, just as they are today. But now, it's the theme-park rides which seem to be the big pull although the zoo still has a variety of animals and birds, including lions, chimps, giraffes, hippos and kangaroos. You can even be a zoo-keeper for a day (for £99). Stamford Bridge vet Matt Brash put the place on a larger map through his Zoo Vet television series. Matt, along with two other vets, took part in castrating one of the stars here last summer. Ernie, a three-year old hippo, required the snip to stop him making advances at his mum, Betty, and his aunt, Godzilla who shared his enclosure. It was the first time such an operation had been attempted in this country. The surgery took six hours and 2020mg of anaesthetic was needed to put Ernie under – enough to knock out 400 men. **DO**

Index